EAST YORKSHIRE VILLAGE VISITS

MARTIN LIMON

FONTHILL

Early in 2007 Roy Woodcock, the editor of The Journal, a Yorkshire county magazine based in Hull, asked me if I would be interested in writing a series called 'village visit'. I eagerly accepted the challenge and decided from the outset that I would focus my attention on social history, personalities, and interesting events to make the series as accessible as possible to the readership of the magazine.

In 2010 Blackthorn Press published my book The Villages of East Yorkshire based on forty of the villages from the early years of the Journal series. This new book is based on studies of thirty-one more villages that appeared in the Journal during 2011, 2012 and 2013.

Martin Limon

Fonthill Media Limited
Fonthill Media LLC
www.fonthillmedia.com
office@fonthillmedia.com

First published in the United Kingdom 2013

British Library Cataloguing in Publication Data:
A catalogue record for this book is available from the British Library

ISBN 978-1-78155-264-3

Typeset in Sabon 9.5/13
Printed and bound in England

Connect with us
facebook.com/fonthillmedia   twitter.com/fonthillmedia

CONTENTS

CHAPTER 1

Goodmanham

For those who enjoy exploring the picturesque villages of East Yorkshire the Yorkshire Wolds settlement of Goodmanham, one mile northeast of Market Weighton, is one of those must-see places in the county for this is a location of national significance in the religious development of Britain. The Anglian place name is thought to be derived from 'the home of Godmund and his people' but the area was probably a centre of worship in prehistoric times. According to Roman writers the inhabitants of Britain worshipped forces of nature like water and the location of several ancient springs here probably meant that this became a sacred place for the worship of pagan deities.

Old cottage at Goodmanham c. 1900. *Image courtesy of Merle Skinner*

The position of the village on a south-facing slope of the Yorkshire Wolds made it ideal for settlement for its fertile land, its plentiful sources of water and an abundant supply of stone for building attracted people from prehistoric times onwards. Archaeological investigations have revealed burial mounds from the Stone Age while the discovery of Samian pottery in the nineteenth century and more recent finds have indicated that this was a favoured location of Romano-Britons too. In the year 2000 archaeologists unearthed a Roman woodworking plane with an ivory stock and iron cutting blade during their excavation of a ditch: the only example of such a tool ever found in Britain.

The departure of the Roman legions by the early fifth century AD left East Yorkshire vulnerable to invasion by Anglo-Saxon tribes from the continent and Goodmanham was just one of the places settled by these newcomers. According to the Christian historian Bede, the village was to play a dramatic part in the conversion of these heathen settlers to Christianity during the reign of King Edwin of Northumbria (586-632). Edwin's palace is thought to have occupied the site of the later Goodmanham Hall while a knoll in the village centre (where the church stands today) is believed to have been the location of a heathen 'temple' dedicated to the worship of the Germanic god Woden and other deities. Bede named 'Coifi' as the chief priest at Goodmanham and described how he and his master, King Edwin, were converted to Christianity (in AD 627) after listening to the preaching of Paulinus, a missionary sent by the Pope. However Edwin had other more practical reasons for supporting the new religion. His new wife, Ethelburga, was a Christian princess from the kingdom of Kent and in those turbulent times of warring and competing Anglo-Saxon kingdoms the king needed allies.

According to Bede's *Ecclesiastical History of England* it was Coifi who took the lead in destroying the pagan 'temple' at Goodmanham. Bede wrote

> As soon as he reached the shrine, he cast into it the spear he carried and thus profaned it. Then he told his companions to set fire to the shrine and its enclosures and destroy them. Here it was that the Chief Priest desecrated and destroyed the altars that he had himself dedicated.

Pope Gregory in AD 601 had established the policy that Christian churches should be built on the sites of former pagan shrines, 'so that the people of the land, acknowledging the true God, may the more familiarly resort to the place to which they have been accustomed.' We can therefore assume that a wooden church was erected at Goodmanham in the years that followed Coifi's destruction of the pagan shrine. The stone-built Norman church of All Hallows dates from around AD 1130 with the nave being built first and the square tower added around fifty years later. In the centuries that followed there were more additions and improvements with for example church bells being installed around 1500.

Goodmanham Windmill in the late nineteenth century. *Image courtesy of Merle Skinner*

Goodmanham Main Street *c.* 1900. *Image courtesy of Merle Skinner*

In isolated and self-supporting farming communities like Goodmanham the church was central to the lives of ordinary folk and the vicar was a figure of both importance and power. Yet sometimes even his moral strictures went unheeded for documents in the East Riding Archive reveal that in 1723 William Clark had privately offered six pounds towards the maintenance of a child he had fathered, 'for he was afraid his wife should hear of it'. The mother of the child was Jane Wallis, a spinster of Goodmanham, and she went on to allege that Clark had tried to bribe her to say that Thomas Bell was the father.

By the nineteenth century education was seen as a way of improving the lives of the labouring poor with the Church of England playing an important part. In a directory of 1823 William Wilson was named as the schoolmaster and the children were taught in the basement of the church tower. Following the enactment of the 1870 Education Act a new purpose-built school was erected two years later with accommodation for fifty children. The log books of Goodmanham Church of England School, held by the East Riding Archive, point to the attendance problems common to many village schools in the nineteenth century when children were expected to undertake farm work. In May 1893 for example the teacher wrote:

Several children are absent working in the fields, some are tending cows and others are picking fruit.

Poor attendance may have been a factor in a critical report of April 1895 when the inspector wrote:

The school has been sadly neglected during the year and is now plainly inefficient. Reading, writing and arithmetic are all very unsatisfactory.

With the threat of the annual government grant being withdrawn it seems that matters improved for after another inspection in February 1898 it was said:

This is in most respects a well taught little county school.

One of the tasks of the vicar of Goodmanham was to make regular visits to the school in order to monitor the work of the children. Around 1898 the Reverend Arthur Braund arrived in the parish to take up this task and by looking at the online census records for Goodmanham we can find out more about him. The 1911 census shows that Braund had been born at Plumsted in Kent and that living with him at the Rectory was his wife Mary, his son Brian and two domestic servants. Braund's son did not attend the village school for the 1911 census tells us that he was being educated at home by his governess: Elsie Alexander, age twenty-four.

It seems that Braund was a kindly well-meaning man for the East Riding school inspector, Mr J. Moffat, said of him in September 1924:

Right: The main road to Market Weighton *c.* 1900. *Image courtesy of Merle Skinner*

Below: A nineteenth-century engraving of the interior of Goodmanham Church. The nave of the church dates from *c.* AD 1130. *Image courtesy of Merle Skinner*

RECTOR'S CIGARS FOR HUNS

A CLERGYMAN'S "POLITE-NESS."

For having given cigars to ten German prisoners who were in the waiting-room at Market Weighton (Yorks) Station the Rev. Arthur George Braund, rector of Goodman-ham (Yorks), England, was fined £3 8/.

It was stated that he went into the waiting-room, and, seeing the prisoners there, he raised his hat to them. After going into the town he returned with some cigars, which he distributed among the prisoners.

In evidence he admitted that the stationmaster told him before he bought the cigars that a woman had been fined £5 for giving cigarettes to prisoners. He went out saying that the armistice had been signed, and that he would get some cigars. People who knew his habits were aware that he treated all alike, and that he raised his hat to the police inspector or the labourer.

Above: The Norman Church of All Hallows is located on a knoll in the centre of the village. It is thought that before AD 627 a pagan open-air 'temple' or enclosure dedicated to Woden occupied the site. This was destroyed by Coifi the high priest of Northumbria after the conversion of King Edwin to Christianity.

Left: The strange case of the Revd Arthur Braund, Rector of Goodmanham, found guilty of 'fraternising' with German prisoners at Market Weighton Railway Station in November 1918. *Taken from an Australian newspaper*

Above: Goodmanham is a popular destination for walkers since the 'Wolds Way' long distance footpath passes through the village.

Right: The Goodmanham Arms public house. It is well known locally for its 'real ales', its microbrewery, its music nights and the quality of its home-cooked food.

The vicar is exceptionally good to the children of this school. He has spent quite a large sum out of his own pocket on improvements to the buildings and keeps the poorer children well supplied with boots and other items during the winter.

Six years earlier Braund's generosity had got him into serious trouble with the law when he appeared in court on a charge of 'fraternising' with the enemy, namely some German POWs, and was fined three guineas plus costs. On 11 November 1918 the First World War had ended but after four years of fighting and millions of deaths anti-German feeling was running high. On 23 November Braund saw ten German prisoners of war under guard at Market Weighton Railway Station and is said to have raised his hat to them before cycling into the town to buy a box of cigars which he then distributed among the prisoners. By way of excuse it was said that the armistice with Germany had been signed and that Braund's 'politeness' was characteristic of the man for 'people who knew his habits were aware that he treated all alike and that he raised his hat to the police inspector or the labourer'.

In the twenty-first century Goodmanham remains an agricultural village with five working farms in the parish. At the time of the 2001 census Goodmanham had a population of just 280 compared to over 300 in the mid nineteenth century. Planning controls mean that new development has been limited and this has helped the village to retain the charm of yesteryear.

CHAPTER 2

Sledmere

On a fine summer's day those heading west from Driffield will see on the top of Garton Hill a huge tower filling the skyline of the Yorkshire Wolds. One hundred and twenty feet tall this Sledmere Monument was built by public subscription in 1865 in honour of Sir Tatton Sykes a larger-than-life figure who ruled this part of East Yorkshire as a kind of benevolent despot in the early nineteenth century.

For over 250 years the Sykes family have dominated the area around Sledmere although the origins of the place are much older for archaeological investigations show that that there was a settlement here in the Stone Age and the Bronze Age. The name Sledmere comes to us from the Anglian and Scandinavian settlers who

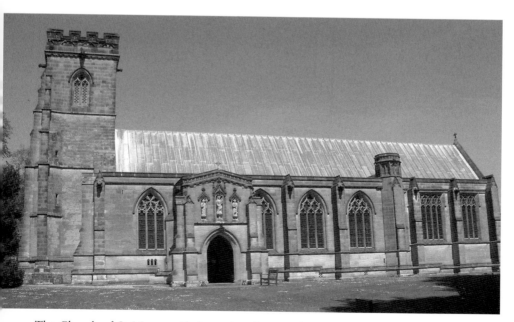

The Church of St Mary at Sledmere has fourteenth-century origins and was largely rebuilt for Sir Tatton Sykes, the fifth baronet, in 1898.

arrived from the fifth century and is derived from the words *slaed* meaning a valley and *marr* meaning a pool. In the Middle Ages Sledmere was a place of some importance for in the fourteenth century it had been granted the right to hold a weekly market and an annual fair. The Norman church and the nearby manor house provided the main focus in medieval times but Richard Sykes and Christopher Sykes demolished much of the old village from the mid-eighteenth century to make way for Sledmere House (1751) and to improve the area surrounding it.

Christopher Sykes (1749-1801) was granted possession of the Sledmere Estate in 1770 and it was he who began the transformation of the countryside around his grand house drawing on the work of the landscape architects Thomas White and Lancelot 'Capability' Brown. Part of his far-reaching schemes to create a beautiful environment in which to live included the planting of trees across a thousand acres and the diversion of the main Bridlington to York road. Sykes also started the new village of Sledmere in 1778 and designed significant farm buildings on the estate. One of these was Life Hill Farm, still an important part of the Sledmere scene today. Fay Grace has lived there since 1998 and told me:

> Set high on the Yorkshire Wolds, Life Hill Farm was always intended to be an eye-catcher. Planned as a model farm by Sir Christopher Sykes the farmhouse was put there so that it could be viewed from Sledmere House but it also enjoys the vista south to the Humber Estuary. The 500 acres of good arable land on which it sits has always been able to support the model farm and the families who live and work there.

In the early nineteenth century Sledmere was typical of most East Riding villages with its population of 425 people dependent on farming and other rural occupations. In 1823 there were nine farmers in the village and in the same year Sir Tatton Sykes, the fourth baronet (1772-1863), succeeded to the Sledmere Estate after the death of his elder brother. As the Sledmere Monument suggests Sir Tatton was a man much revered and in his lifetime it was claimed that in his long-frock coat, frilled shirt, breeches and high boots he was along with York Minster and Fountains Abbey one of the three great sights of Yorkshire. Not a great scholar Sir Tatton's main interests were boxing, agricultural improvement and breeding horses. His interest in horseracing meant that by the time of his death in 1863 the Sledmere Stud numbered around 300 thoroughbreds.

Sir Tatton was a man with the common touch and made no distinction between the various classes he met for farmers and tradesmen were equally as welcome at Sledmere as his more exalted guests. Yet while he was a charming and generous host to others with his own family he could be a bully and a brute for he ruled over them with the 'vicious rage of a stone-age tyrant' and subjected his sons to regular beatings for the flimsiest of excuses. His own wife hid herself away in the

Right: Situated on Garton Hill, Sledmere Monument is a 120-foot tall tower built in 1865 in honour of Sir Tatton Sykes, the fourth baronet of Sledmere. It was paid for by public subscription among those 'who loved him as a friend and honoured him as a landlord'. Around the monument there are various sculpted scenes of Sir Tatton in his everyday life on the estate.

Below: Richard Sykes began building Sledmere House in 1751 demolishing some of the old village houses to improve its setting. Two further wings were added by Sir Christopher Sykes and he commissioned the plasterer Joseph Rose to decorate the interiors. Set in 2,000 acres of parkland and gardens, Sledmere House is one of East Yorkshire's premier visitor attractions.

Sledmere orangery when she was at home and escaped to London whenever she could.

Growing up in 'an atmosphere devoid of love' it is not surprising that his eldest son was a shy withdrawn figure and renowned for his eccentric behaviour. Sir Tatton Sykes, the fifth baronet (1826-1913) believed that the body should be kept at a constant temperature so he would wear six overcoats and two pairs of trousers discarding layers only when it became necessary. Other aspects of his bizarre behaviour were his love of milk puddings, his dislike of flowers and his prejudice against women gossiping on front doorsteps. He therefore built estate houses without front doors. In April 1869 a local newspaper reported that he was determined to stop 'the practice of stick gathering' and insisted on the prosecution of two local women who had trespassed in Croome Wood for that purpose. On a more positive note this Sledmere grandee had a long-term interest in church architecture and during his lifetime he is said to have spent £1.5 million on church building and restoration projects in the East Riding including those at Garton-on-the-Wolds and Wetwang. He also set about the improvement of Sledmere itself by building new terraced houses, a new schoolhouse and a post office.

In 1874 Sir Tatton Sykes was pressured into marrying Christina Cavendish-Bentinck a woman thirty years his junior and although she gave him one son (Sir Mark Sykes, the sixth baronet) the union was not a happy one. By the 1890s she was leading a separate life in London and running up large debts that Sir Tatton eventually refused to honour.

When Sir Tatton died in 1913 his vast Yorkshire estates passed to his son, Mark, who had already led an adventurous life as a traveller and a soldier fighting in the Boer War. Those who have visited Sledmere will have seen a monument closely associated with his military career, the Waggoner's Memorial designed by him and erected in 1919. The memorial is a tribute to a thousand young farm workers from among his tenants in the East Riding who in 1912-1913 answered his call to form a reserve regiment of those skilled in driving horse-drawn wagons. They were paid a pound a year as a 'retainer' for Sykes was convinced that a European war was looming and that the specialist skills of the waggoners would be a useful asset to the British Army. In the event he was proved correct for in August 1914 the First World War broke out and his men were among the first to see action in France and Belgium.

The circular twenty foot high Portland stone monument is unique among war memorials in Britain for its carved scenes tell the story of the waggoners from the outbreak of war when they were working in the fields at harvest time to their arrival in France and conflict with the Germans. Across the road at Sledmere House is a fascinating free museum with photographs and memorabilia that further explores the remarkable exploits of these brave soldiers.

The picturesque village with its distinctive estate houses, its church and its wonderful monuments has long been a popular destination for sightseers and in the

A drawing of Sir Tatton Sykes (1772-1863), the fourth baronet who began Sledmere's long association with horse racing. One of his boasts was that he seen the St Ledger on seventy-four consecutive occasions.

The Triton Inn was built in the 1780s and was formerly a coaching inn. It was part of the new village of Sledmere created by Sir Christopher Sykes.

The Wolds Waggoner's Memorial stands alongside the main road through the village. Erected in 1919 its various sculpted scenes tell the story of this remarkable reserve regiment. The inscriptions says:

Lieutenant Colonel Sir Mark Sykes Baronet MP designed this monument and set it up as a remembrance of the calling and services rendered in the great war 1914-1919 by the Wolds Waggoner's Reserve, a corps of 1000 drivers raised by him on the Yorkshire Wolds Farms in the year 1912.

Sir Mark Sykes, the sixth baronet, succeeded to the Sledmere Estate in 1913. He was a politician, soldier and diplomatic advisor to the British Government on Middle East affairs. He died in France in 1919 during the great influenza pandemic that killed fifty million people worldwide. During the avian 'flu scare of 2007 permission was given for the removal of tissue samples from his grave to aid medical research.

A postcard view of Sledmere village *c.* 1900.

1920s Lady Sykes (the widow of Sir Mark) remarked that Sledmere 'had become on Sundays a sort of holiday resort for charabanc and motor car holiday parties'. Sledmere House itself began to open to the public on a regular basis in 1964 and by 2005 was attracting around 20,000 visitors a year. Restored after a disastrous fire in 1911 the house is a Grade I listed building containing Chippendale, Sheraton and other fine furniture together with many beautiful paintings. Among its many rooms are the 'Long Library' said to be the most beautiful room in England and the 'Turkish Room' inspired by Sir Mark's travels in the Middle East and based on a design in the Yeni Mosque in Istanbul.

With its superb setting, a planned layout, and a uniformity of character it is easy to understand the continuing attraction of Sledmere. Unlike other East Riding settlements the village remains unspoilt by change and it is not surprising that with its wealth of listed buildings was granted 'conservation area' status as early as 1974.

CHAPTER 3

Gilberdyke

The completion of the M62 motorway with the opening of the Ouse Bridge in May 1976 was an important event in the history of East Yorkshire not only for motorists using it but also for the residents of Newport and Gilberdyke who gained some respite from the heavy traffic of former times. Anyone who has visited these two villages will have noticed how superior their main road is compared to other places in the East Riding. What is now the quieter B1230 route was once part of the busy Liverpool-Leeds-Hull trunk road. Plans and contracts in Beverley's Treasure House show how in the 1950s the East Riding County Council brought about improvements to this vital route, then part of the A63.

The main road through Gilberdyke was once part of the busy Liverpool – Leeds – Hull Trunk Road (the A63).

Transport has long been an important factor in the development of Gilberdyke, sixteen miles west of Hull, for the name of the village is derived from 'Gilbert's Dyke', a waterway sixteen feet wide and eight feet deep, completed in the twelfth century to connect the River Foulness to the River Ouse at Blacktoft. Gilbert Hansard was given land here in 1154 by the Bishop of Durham and it was he who had the dyke built to drain the surrounding marshes, to power a watermill and provide a trade route navigable by boats. It was at the point where the dyke crossed the Howden to North Cave road that the settlement of Gilberdyke developed.

For much of its history Gilberdyke, like other places in the East Riding, would have been dominated by the needs of farming. Until enclosure in 1830 there were three open arable fields together with the large expanse of Wallingfen Common used for summer grazing, for winter fodder and for catching game and fish. In a directory of 1823 Isaac Hairsine and four other farmers were named and they would have employed many others from Gilberdyke's population of over three hundred people to carry out the labour intensive work of the time.

Another name included in the directory was William Lawton who was an Overseer of the Poor. Under the Elizabethan poor laws each parish was responsible for the maintenance of paupers who for reasons like unemployment, ill health or old age could not support themselves. In February 1837 Gilberdyke became one of the forty parishes of the Howden Poor Law Union and accommodation in a well-regulated workhouse became the preferred way of dealing with paupers. A new workhouse was built at Howden in 1839 and the ratepayers of Gilberdyke had to contribute to the cost of running it.

The elected Board of Guardians who supervised the system of poor relief both inside the workhouse and outside it were anxious to minimise the cost and this is reflected in both their minute books and their correspondence. A minute of the 22 February 1840 for example ordered that their clerk should write to Mr John Gardham, 'requiring him to maintain his mother Mary Gardham belonging to Gilberdyke'. Absent fathers were also a target of the Guardians and in January 1841 they decided to apply to a magistrate for an order against Joseph Rose a farm labourer for 'the maintenance of a male bastard child of Mary Briskhane born on the 8 December 1840 and chargeable to Gilberdyke'.

Occasionally the Howden Guardians decided to act with greater humanity and from a letter of the 9 December 1842 in the East Riding Archive we learn that George Caville of Gilberdyke would be supported because:

The pauper is seventy-seven years of age, his wife has recently died and that the old man being thus left alone is desirous of living with his son instead of in the workhouse.

Anxious to remain within the law the guardians were also forced to consult with the Poor Law Board in London on other issues. In April 1844 they asked for

The White Horse Inn once catered for the drovers and lorry drivers using the main road through the village.

Jubilee Pond at Gilberdyke was once the pond for the flax mill (now demolished). The pond was officially named The Jubilee Pond during the Queen's Silver Jubilee Celebrations in 1977.

clarification about the case of Thomas Craven, his sister and her two children who were Americans by birth but had come to live with their brother, Charles Craven, a Gilberdyke farmer. Subsequently Charles Craven had moved away and abandoned them leaving the four to be supported by the parish. The Howden Guardians wanted to know if they could legally assist them to return to America.

While fear of destitution and the workhouse remained a powerful influence among the working classes in the nineteenth century at least new employment opportunities arose with the arrival of the railway. Gilberdyke was one of the first places in the East Riding to be served when the Selby to Hull Railway opened on the 1 July 1840 while in 1869 a link west of Gilberdyke Station, then called Staddlethorpe, provided a route to Goole, Doncaster and London. By the 1870s there was also a railway siding to a flax mill here built by Edward Oliver a local farmer. Flax was used for making linen and other products and about 300 acres of this locally grown crop were processed at the mill until it closed around 1930.

Bulmer's Directory of 1892 shows us that in the late nineteenth century the needs of Gilberdyke's population was served by tradesmen typical of any self-contained village at that time including a shoemaker, a wheelwright, a blacksmith and a builder. The builder in question was George Dodsworth and he also operated the public house called Wards Hotel. Thirsty local people and a brisk passing trade on the main road also supported the Rose and Crown public house and the Cross Keys.

The building of a new school in 1895 providing an elementary education up to the age of twelve indicates the growing importance of Gilberdyke. In 1918 the school leaving age was raised to fourteen and from inspection reports held at the East Riding Archive in Beverley we can learn a great deal about Gilberdyke School in the 1920s and 1930s. When Mr J. Moffat visited the school in June 1921 he reported that there were one hundred and seventy seven children on roll taught by five staff and a student trainee. Moffat was complimentary about its hard-working headmaster, Mr Appleton, who 'conveys the impression of being a well-balanced schoolmaster exercising a good general supervision'.

In the days before free school transport Moffat's reports also indicate the effort required by Gilberdyke's pupils to get to school for he said:

Many pupils live about two miles away and several others walk over three miles to get there.

Yet not every Gilberdyke parent was impressed with what it had to offer. In November 1926 Moffat interviewed a mother living at Clementhorpe House in the village. She was teaching her child at home with a view to sending her to a private school in Goole because she, 'does not wish her child to mix with the children at the elementary school'.

The school buildings were also of concern with the use of open fires for heating being an issue while in 1935 Moffat commented that heavy traffic on the main

Gilberdyke Station (originally called Staddlethorpe) was opened in 1840. The track here and at Staddlethorpe Junction was the scene of several accidents. On the 7 March 1875 an express train left the tracks near the station while on the 13 February 1872 at Staddlethorpe Junction there was a collision between a passenger train and a portion of a goods train.

New housing close to Gilberdyke Station occupied land that was once part of Staddlethorpe.

Gilberdyke Windmill *c.* 1910.
*Image courtesy of the East
Riding Museums Service*

road had led to 'high undulations' in the classroom floors. It was perhaps with some relief that in 1972 East Riding County Council began the building of a new school in Scalby Lane.

Today this caters for around 300 pupils and in 2008 was judged by the Office for Standards in Education to be an 'outstanding school providing an exceedingly effective environment for pupils to mature into well rounded individuals with a thirst for learning'. As well as praising the work of the school in reading, writing and mathematics the OFSTED inspection was complimentary about its excellent range of clubs providing 'extra opportunities for pupils to enjoy exercise and sport'.

Like many East Riding villages in the last forty years Gilberdyke has seen a rapid expansion and at the time of the 2001 census had a population of over 3,000 people. Large numbers of new houses have been built while employment opportunities have been created by an industrial estate built on former railway sidings.

CHAPTER 4

Langtoft

For those who regularly use the Driffield to Scarborough route via Staxton Hill the picturesque village of Langtoft, nestling in a dry valley high in the Yorkshire Wolds six miles north of Driffield, will be a familiar sight. As you descend Tye How Hill the B1249 road twists and turns through the narrow main street of this ancient community. The name of the place is thought to be derived from the Norse words *lang* (meaning long) and *toft* (site of a house) but archaeological discoveries show that there was settlement here before the Scandinavian invasions of eastern England in the ninth century. In September 2000, for example, metal detector enthusiasts uncovered two hoards of Roman coins dating from the early

The main street of Langtoft forms part of the B1249 road.

fourth century on farmland near the village. Around 1,900 silver coins were found in two earthenware pots and were subsequently declared 'treasure' at a Hull coroner's inquest. Sold at auction in 2002 the coins attracted attention from collectors all over the world and netted the lucky finders and the Langtoft farmer over £16,000.

In most East Riding villages the church is often the oldest surviving structure and Langtoft is no exception. Parts of the church of St Peter date back to the thirteenth century but there was much rebuilding in the nineteenth century. In the Middle Ages those of humble origins but with talent and ambition often saw the church as the way to education and advancement. One of Langtoft's claims to fame was that it was the birthplace of Peter de Langtoft a noted medieval scholar and historian of the thirteenth century. He was an Augustinian monk at Bridlington Priory and wrote *Langtoft's Chronicle*, a history of England in Anglo-Norman verse. Although little is known about his life Langtoft must have been a talented individual for until 1286 he represented Bridlington Priory in a series of negotiations at Westminster and elsewhere. Peter de Langtoft died around 1305 but in celebration of his life and work Sir Tatton Sykes erected a memorial in the early twentieth century. The Langtoft Cross stands on a small green at the southern end of the village and depicts Peter de Langtoft being taken by his father to be educated by the monks of Bridlington Priory.

By the time that Edward Baines wrote about Langtoft in the 1820s the village population stood at around 400 people and in common with other villages most would have been engaged in farming or other rural occupations. Thirteen farmers were named in his directory of 1823 and also living there were the usual tradesmen of the time like a blacksmith, three shoemakers and two tailors. The 1861 census provides us with further details of the inhabitants. Living at Bleak House was Henry Wilson, a farmer of seventy-six acres, his wife, his two sons, his eighteen-year-old house servant Mary Warrington and Richard Leason a twenty-nine-year-old agricultural labourer. Living on Front Street was a shoemaker called Thomas Hill, his wife, his six children and two other shoemakers employed in the business.

Also living on Langtoft's main street, through probably in more humble circumstances, was William Mason an agricultural labourer and his wife Mary. From a local newspaper we learn that she was the victim, six years later, of a vicious assault by a young woman 'rejoicing in the name of Jane Ann Slaughter'. The newspaper story said that Mary Mason was talking to the defendant's mother when Jane Slaughter came rushing out of her house 'using an epithet which only vulgar mouths can utter, sprang upon the complainant, dealt her a terrific blow on the chest and continued striking the poor woman on various parts of the body until she fell to the ground insensible and bleeding like a stuck sheep'. Having listened to the case local magistrates decided to fine Jane Slaughter five pounds plus costs but when she refused to pay they sent her to the Beverley House of Correction for a month instead.

Above: This marble plaque near the junction of Front Street and Back Street records the Great Floods of 1657 and 1892.

Left: The Langtoft Cross was paid for by the Sledmere grandee Sir Tatton Sykes and commemorates the life of Peter de Langtoft, medieval scholar and historian. It stood close to Low Mere one of Langtoft's two village ponds.

St Peter's Church at Langtoft dates from the thirteenth century.

The Ship Inn at Langtoft. In a directory of 1823 it was called the Nelson.

The George and Dragon pub *c.* 1905 when George Cleminson was the licensee. *Image courtesy of www.paul-gibson.com*

The Langtoft village pond *c.* 1910. This was filled in *c.* 1960. *Image courtesy of www. paul-gibson.com*

'Blackcock' is the work of the talented Langtoft artist John Naylor. *Image courtesy of John Naylor*

From the evidence of the same newspaper Langtoft seems to have had a problem with feisty females for it reported on similar cases of assault in 1871 and 1873. Drunkenness was also an issue brought before magistrates and centred on Langtoft's two public houses, the Ship and the George and Dragon. In 1882 John Elvidge was charged after being found 'very drunk and bawling in the street with two men holding him up' while in 1886 George Dennis was fined five shillings for being 'beastly drunk at Langtoft and going about the streets cursing and swearing'. In 1893 the landlord of the George and Dragon public house, Edward Rawlinson, was himself the victim of a drunken assault by one of his customers, John Elvidge. Rawlinson was so badly beaten that he was 'delirious for four or five nights' and lost the sight of his left eye. He sued Elvidge for £25 damages while magistrates too were determined to punish the perpetrator by fining him £12 10s 0d.

Walking around this tranquil Wolds community today it is difficult to imagine its more turbulent past or indeed the natural calamities that have beset the village over the centuries. One reminder however is a marble plaque set in the wall of a cottage recording the 'Great Floods of Langtoft' of 1657 and 1892. Situated in a valley surrounded on three sides by hills makes the village particularly susceptible to flooding after heavy rain and the plaque only tells part of the story. Another of Langtoft's weather calamities was in December 1874 when a storm completely demolished the Wesleyan Chapel then under construction while in July 1876 the cross on the eastern end of the parish church was torn off by a bolt of lightning also damaging brickwork and the roof. The year 1888 was another disastrous one for Langtoft for on 9 June heavy rainfall led to a torrent of floodwater forty feet wide swamping the lower parts of the village. The residents took refuge in the upper rooms of their cottages while the deluge flooded the ground floors to a depth of four feet bursting open doors and carrying away 'pots, pans, chairs stools and mats'.

Four years later Langtoft was struck by the 'Great Flood of 3 July 1892'. A contemporary account records that an electrical storm approached around 7 p.m. with immense hailstones and a cloud burst displacing chalk from the surrounding hillsides. The storm water then entered the village at Westgate inundating a row of twelve chalk cottages before sweeping down to swamp the joiner's shop of Henry Woodmansey on Back Street completely destroying it and washing away his tools. On this occasion it was the sheer force of the floods that devastated Langtoft and villagers were forced to take refuge in St Peter's Church until they subsided.

While Langtoft continues to be a victim of the weather (with more flooding in June 2007 and July 2009) it retains a tremendous sense of identity, community and enterprise. With a good mix of old and new properties Langtoft is an attractive place to live and the list of village facilities and activities is impressive. Langtoft's church, the village pub, the Old Mill hotel with bar and restaurant, the Children's Centre and the bowls club are all facets of a thriving community.

CHAPTER 5

Bishop Wilton

To the south of Garrowby Hill in a valley cut into the lower slopes of the Yorkshire Wolds lies the lovely village of Bishop Wilton (four miles north of Pocklington) with a stream of crystal clear water running through the centre of it. Wide grass verges and eighteenth and nineteenth century cottages border Bishop Wilton Beck and it is not surprising that this beautiful and unique place was first designated as a conservation area in 1974. Archaeological discoveries like artefacts and funeral barrows show that the area has been a place of habitation since the Stone Age while the name of the village seems to come from the time of the Anglo-Scandinavian invasions of eastern England after the departure of the Romans.

The Bishop Wilton Beck and wide grass verges make the village one of the prettiest in the East Riding.

Originally called 'Wilton' the village probably took its name from the Old English word *wiell* (a spring) while *ton* meant an enclosed homestead. The prefix 'Bishop' was not added until after the Norman Conquest and recognises that from the thirteenth century the village became the site of a palace of the Archbishop of York. Members of the Bishop Wilton Local History Group have undertaken considerable research on the subject and this suggests that the palace was built at the time of Walter de Gray, Archbishop of York from 1216 to 1245. Covering nine acres the moated site encompassed a range of buildings, two fishponds, a millpond and a dovecote while parkland to the east and south of it was probably used for hunting deer and rabbits. The moat surrounding the palace is still visible on three sides although the buildings themselves had a relatively short life for by 1377 it was said that they 'were in a very ruinous state and almost fallen down'. Exactly why the palace was abandoned is still a matter of debate but one reason may have been more difficult economic circumstances following the outbreak of the Black Death in the mid fourteenth century.

Disease was a problem that continued to afflict the village in the centuries that followed for until comparatively recently medicine had few answers on either the causes of illnesses or their cure. The logbooks of Bishop Wilton School, held by the East Riding Archive in Beverley, provide evidence of the medical uncertainties of life in the nineteenth century for in July 1863 the schoolmaster wrote:

> John Johnson is detained at home under suspicion of his having the smallpox which is prevalent in the village.

A rather distressed schoolmaster was also able to reflect on his own personal sorrow at the premature death of a close friend in 1876. On 26 May he wrote:

> The school closed on Tuesday and Wednesday of this week in consequence of my attending the funeral of our beloved friend Miss Askwith of Weaverthorpe. The journey, so full of melancholy, was to me a striking lesson and warning. A young lady in the prime of life endowed with all that was virtuous and amiable cut down by the cold hand of death.

In the nineteenth century farming and other rural occupations remained the mainstay of the local economy. In a directory of 1823 eleven farmers and yeomen were listed for Bishop Wilton while the rural economy also supported a corn miller, a blacksmith, a carpenter and three public houses. Census returns provide further details of the inhabitants and that taken in 1871 shows the presence at the Fleece Inn of Thomas Dales (innkeeper and bricklayer), his wife Mary, his three sons, his two daughters and his general servant Maria Wake. One of the village blacksmiths of that year was John Ellis, aged sixty-four and another person named was his eighteen-year-old apprentice William Cook.

Above: The Fleece Inn at Bishop Wilton. In a directory of 1892 John Elsworth was the licensee.

Right: The Church of St Edith is one of the East Riding's most beautiful churches and was restored in 1859 at the expense of Sir Tatton Sykes.

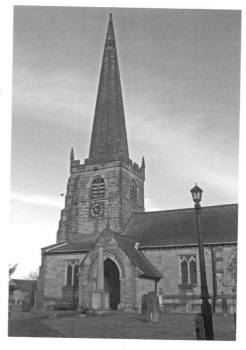

At harvest time the whole community was expected to play its part and this both determined the timing of school holidays and provided the 'excuse' for absenteeism at other times. On 18 July 1873 the schoolmaster wrote:

> The attendance is still very thin. Turnip hoeing keeps many children from school.

Less than a month later he was anticipating the imminent arrival of the summer holidays when he wrote:

> The harvest is making its approach but it will probably be two weeks before vacation commences.

From entries in the school log book it is clear that some pupils and parents were not prepared to wait for the official holidays to begin. On 2 July 1877 an exasperated schoolmaster commented:

> There are many of the children working out in the fields and doing it without a farming certificate.

According to a local history of the village the school had been erected at the expense of Sir Tatton Sykes in 1868 but subsequent reports show it was not the most luxurious or convenient of buildings. On 17 March 1876 the schoolmaster wrote in the logbook:

> The cold winds make the children uncomfortable at their work. I have frequently to stop work and clap hands.

At that time coal fires provided heating but the pupils were expected to pay for the privilege! In October 1873 the schoolmaster wrote that some of the children had been rather 'dilatory' in paying their 'coal money' and that only those who had paid 'should be allowed to go near the fire'.

These problems persisted into the twentieth century with a government inspector commenting in the late 1920s on the difficulty of teaching two different classes in the main room without a dividing screen. When the East Riding Schools' Inspector, Mr J. Moffat, visited Bishop Wilton in September 1929 he reported:

> Nothing has been done with regard to improved heating and much discomfort was experienced last winter.

By the late 1920s Bishop Wilton School had around seventy pupils on roll and although Moffat was satisfied with the teaching he commented, in his usual blunt

The new Bishop Wilton Community Hall was funded in part by the National Lottery and opened in 2010.

Pupils of Bishop Wilton School in 1928 with their headmaster Edgar Dearnley. *Image courtesy of the Bishop Wilton Local History Group*

The centre of the village *c.* 1900. *Image courtesy of the Bishop Wilton Local History Group*

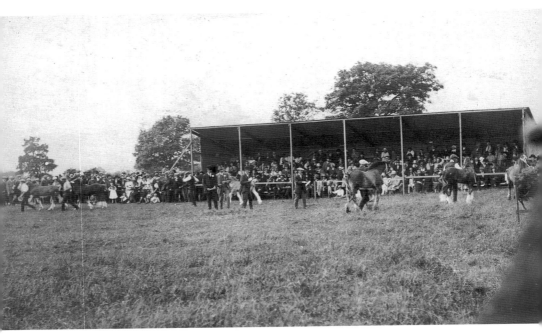

The Bishop Wilton Show of 1923. *Image courtesy of the Bishop Wilton Local History Group*

Inside the horticulture tent at the Bishop Wilton Show, July 2010. *Image courtesy of Derek Thomas*

manner, 'the school possesses more than its fair share of dull and mentally deficient children'. (October 1934).

Today the school is part of an active and thriving community and one of the important events in the village social calendar is the Bishop Wilton Show and Craft Fair held in July each year. The origins of the event can be traced back to 1897 when a group of local people met together in the schoolroom to organise the Bishop Wilton Floral and Agricultural Show offering over nine pounds in prizes. A newspaper report on the success of the first show on 2 August 1897 said:

> The exhibits shown were very creditable to the village, the farm produce especially causing the judge some trouble in giving his awards. Winter onions were an excellent class, and eggs very good.
>
> With brass band music, a cricket match and an evening dance this first Bishop Wilton Show became an inspiration to the organisers in the years that followed.

For anyone who has never seen it Bishop Wilton therefore remains one of the 'jewels' of East Yorkshire and well worth a visit. On a warm sunny day it's picturesque setting, its lovely beck, its historic church of St Edith and its wealth of old cottages make Bishop Wilton a truly magical village.

CHAPTER 6

Bugthorpe

In a county with a wealth of attractive-sounding place names, like Swanland and Cherry Burton, to modern ears the name Bugthorpe, twelve miles east of York, does not seem particularly appealing. Yet those who visit this ancient community, part of the Halifax Estate, nestling amid the hills of the Yorkshire Wolds might be surprised to find that Bugthorpe is a very pretty village indeed. With just forty-four dwellings, many built of hand-made bricks and red pantile roofs, clustered around the village green the community seems to be a place lost in time. At the western end of the village stands the most dominant building, the Church of St Andrew, dating from before the Norman Conquest. Although the derivation of the place-name remains a controversial subject it is likely that the origin of Bugthorpe was as a Norse settlement following the Scandinavian invasions of England from the ninth century. *Bugg* was probably the name of one of these Norse settlers while *thorpe* indicates a hamlet or farm. At the time of the Domesday Survey of 1086 the settlement here was called 'Bugtorp' with the King, the Archbishop of York and Odo the Crossbowman being the landowners. Despite an attempt in the

A tranquil scene near Bugthorpe's village green on a Spring day. The Halifax Estate Office is on the right.

nineteenth century to rename it 'Buckthorpe' the original name persists.

Like most East Riding villages until the late eighteenth century the lives of Bugthorpe's population would have been dominated by the needs of farming and the care of crops and animals under a communal system of open fields and pastures. From around 1750, to improve agricultural efficiency, the chief landowners of the East Riding had acts of parliament drawn up which redistributed the medieval strips of land into compact farms where new farming methods could be introduced. At Bugthorpe this process began with an enclosure act passed in 1777.

In a directory of 1823 fourteen farmers were named and they in turn would have employed many 'landless labourers' to carry out the routine tasks of sowing, weeding, harvesting and animal husbandry. One of Bugthorpe's farming families were the Bottrill's and John Bottrill was named in the 1823 directory while at nearby York Matthew Bottrill, gentleman, was living at the prestigious address of Monkgate. Shortly before his death in 1827 Matthew Bottrill made a will in which he said:

> I give to the churchwardens and overseers of the poor of the parish of Bugthorpe (where I was born) the sum of ten pounds to be distributed in money amongst such of the poor inhabitants residing therein as the said churchwardens and overseers shall deem the most deserving objects of charity.

The bulk of Botterill's £30,000 estate however was left to his great nephew, George Hudson, a twenty-seven-year-old York linen draper. Exactly how he came to inherit this money remains a controversial subject since Matthew Botterill had closer relatives and had changed his will in favour of Hudson only weeks before his death. Whatever the truth of later accusations about his inheritance Hudson used the money to good effect to establish a major presence in the 'railway revolution' taking place at the time. He bought shares in the North Midland Railway Company and went on to become a promoter of railways linking York with the West Riding and Newcastle-upon-Tyne. By 1845 Hudson's companies controlled over a thousand miles of railways and he was known as the 'Railway King'. However as investigations showed his success had been achieved by sharp practice such as bribing MPs to persuade them to support his new railway schemes and paying share dividends out of the capital subscribed for new projects. As details of his financial malpractice became known he had to resign from his railway company directorships and was forced to agree to pay back money to shareholders who he had swindled. Later imprisoned for debt his significant contribution was to use his promotional skills to establish York as a major hub of railway development in Britain.

For the poor of Bugthorpe in the nineteenth century, as Matthew Botterill's bequest reveals, much depended on the charitable generosity of wealthier

The Church of St Andrew. There are carvings on the chancel arch that date back to the eleventh century. The earliest of the three bells was cast in 1590.

Bugthorpe shop and post office. Robert Crow, postmaster, is also a respected local artist.

inhabitants and the support of the overseers of the poor. These unpaid officials collected a local property tax called a poor rate for the support of those who because of factors like old age or infirmity could not support themselves. From 1836 Bugthorpe became one of the forty-seven parishes of the Pocklington Poor Law Union and after the erection there of a new workhouse in 1852 'indoor relief' became the preferred way of dealing with paupers seeking help from the parish. Under the guidance of regulations from the Poor Law Board in London life in the workhouse was often hard and unpleasant and was seen as a way of deterring only the most desperate from applying. Census records show that Bugthorpe residents fell prey to the workhouse regime of a strict segregation of the sexes, a limited diet and hard monotonous work. The 1881 census for example reveals the presence at the workhouse of Bugthorpe resident Elizabeth Weatherill, a widow aged seventy-seven together with Louisa Waterson, a twenty-seven-year-old former domestic servant and her three children.

Although the day-to-day running of the Pocklington Workhouse was entrusted to a paid master and matron general supervision was the responsibility of a board of guardians selected from the constituent parishes of the union. In 1897 the representative for Bugthorpe was Samuel Flint, a member of a long established farming family in the parish. Samuel Flint occupied the Manor House and the 1891 census provides us with details of the people living there. In addition to Samuel Flint his wife and three children were a groom, two servants and six of his in-laws.

Along with other places in the East Riding, like Warter, Sledmere and Brantingham, Bugthorpe is essentially an 'estate' village with the majority of properties owned by Halifax Estates. Bugthorpe is part of their Garrowby Estate of 13,500 acres located on the edge of the Yorkshire Wolds escarpment. The village's association with the Halifax family began in 1838 when the Church of England sold all the church lands and the Manor of Bugthorpe to Sir Francis Wood, an ancestor of the present Earl of Halifax. The village benefited from the fact that the first Earl of Halifax, a high-ranking politician of the 1930s and 1940s, lived at nearby Garrowby Hall until his death in 1959.

With the downturn in agriculture in recent times the Halifax Estate has found new tenants for redundant farm buildings and these days Bugthorpe has an enviable reputation for nurturing skilled artists and craftsmen. One of the most famous is Albanian-born sculptor Andrian Melka who established his studio at Bugthorpe in 2003. These days his accomplishments as a sculptor are highly regarded throughout the world and he has worked on projects in the USA as well as for prestigious clients like the Prince of Wales and Lord Rothschild.

At the time of the first census in 1801 Bugthorpe had a population of 244 souls but 200 years later this had fallen to just 122. Despite this Bugthorpe remains a very desirable place to live having escaped the ravages of modern development that have blighted the character of villages elsewhere.

Above: Bugthorpe is a linear village. At the east end of the village the green is 'stopped' by cottages and farm buildings built in the late eighteenth century and early nineteenth century.

Left: Andrian Melka at work on a Venus sculpture at his Bugthorpe studio. *Image courtesy of Andrian Melka*

Andrian Melka working on the Spirit of the Ocean fountain at Santa Barbara, California. *Image courtesy of Andrian Melka*

'Bugthorpe to the West' — a painting by artist Robert Crow. *Image courtesy of Robert Crow*

'Garrowby Hill Crucifix' — a painting by artist Robert Crow. *Image courtesy of Robert Crow*

Bugthorpe is an estate village of Lord Halifax. The first Earl of Halifax lived at nearby Garrowby Hall and was Foreign Secretary in the government of Neville Chamberlain from 1938 to 1940. He is shown here with Germany's Hermann Goering in November 1937.

Apart from hosting Hermann Goering, Lord Halifax had many other official duties. On 11 January 1939 he was at the Teatro dell'Opera di Roma. From left to right: Neville Chamberlain, Benito Mussolini, Lord Halifax, and Mussolini's son-in-law and foreign minister, Count Galeazzo Ciano

CHAPTER 7

Burstwick

Set in gently undulating countryside Burstwick seems to be one of those 'back-of-beyond' places so typical of remote parts of Holderness in that it lies on a 'B' route north of the main Hull to Withernsea road. Often referred to as Skeckling-cum-Burstwick in the nineteenth century it was effectively two settlements separated by Skeckling Drain but gradually the name Burstwick took precedence for the whole of it. The name probably comes to us from the Scandinavians who settled in East Yorkshire from the ninth century and is thought to mean 'Brusti's Dairy Farm.'

Mentioned in the *Domesday Book* (1086) as Brostewic the land was given by King William after the Norman Conquest to one of his chief supporters Drogo de

Main Street and Church Lane Burstwick.

la Beauvriere and by about AD 1200 the Manor of Burstwick was the hub of the estates of the Lords of Holderness. The former importance of their manor house at Burstwick is indicated by the 1855 Ordnance Survey map of the area which shows earthworks indicating a moat and fishponds. Sometimes referred to as 'Burstwick Castle' it consisted of a timber-built hall, chapels and other buildings and was by the end of the thirteenth century a royal residence. King Edward the First stayed here several times during his campaigns to subjugate Scotland. Another famous 'guest' was Elizabeth, wife of Robert the Bruce, who was imprisoned here for about a year in 1308. According to *Bulmer's Directory* (1892) the king entrusted her care at 'Burstwick Castle' to Richard Oysel, steward of the royal manor of Holderness. He was given strict instructions as to her treatment including the provision of two women from her own country to wait upon her and she was to have 'as much venison and fish as she should desire'.

By the 1520s the house was said to be 'utterly in decay' and was rebuilt in stone. By 1802 this too was gone and these days all that exists to remind us of the past glories of the site are the earthworks at South Park on the road to Hedon. In its absence the oldest surviving structure in this very modern village is the Church of All Saints dating from the twelfth to the fourteenth century. When Edward Baines wrote about Burstwick in 1823 he named William Clarke as the vicar and Clarke was to remain the clergyman there until his death in 1852. One of his letters survives in the East Riding Archive in Beverley and reveals something of the strict morality of the man. In 1813 Clarke had been approached by local resident William Vicarman to ask if the clergyman would provide a letter of recommendation for the drinks licence that he was seeking from local magistrates. Clarke wrote:

> It is needless to say that I declined. My objection was not to the man but the measure. There is already one public house in the village and the multiplication of public houses would have a pernicious influence on the morality of the lower classes of society.

The 1851 census shows that William Clarke had been born in Hull, was unmarried and now aged eighty-six. The census also reveals the importance of farming in mid-nineteenth century Burstwick and among the households listed was that of John Sharp, a fifty-two year old farm labourer, his wife and two daughters. At the other end of the social scale and living at Burstwick Grange was Abraham Leonard (fifty-four) a farmer of 435 acres employing five labourers. Along with members of his family the census entry for the house includes the names of seven servants. All of them had cause to celebrate on 13 December 1855 when the marriage of his second daughter, Elizabeth, to Robert Briggs of Sunderland took place at All Saint's Church. An article in a Hull newspaper of the time recorded that the father of the bride 'gave an excellent entertainment to all his servants and labourers' to mark the event.

Above: Main Street Burstwick near Woolam Hill

Left: The War Memorial near Pinfold Lane at Burstwick

While the wedding of Elizabeth Leonard represented one of the happier events in the history of Burstwick life there could be hard and full of uncertainties. Local newspapers reported on cases of 'cattle plague' at Burstwick in 1866-1867 with the animals being put down to prevent the spread of the infection. For ordinary residents too in the days before the Welfare State the death or sickness of a bread-winner or their inability to work because of old age remained a major worry.

In the last resort the poor could look to the parish for support and in common with other East Riding villages Burstwick had its 'overseers of the poor' to provide 'outdoor relief' to paupers. An eighteenth century account book survives in the East Riding Archive to show us both the money collected from ratepayers and the sums paid out to the needy. An entry of 30 March 1724 showed that a total of £1 15s 6d had been disbursed including a payment of nine shillings to 'Blind Jerry'. For those who turned to crime to supplement their earnings the penal code of the time could be extremely harsh and the records of the East Riding Quarter Sessions show that at Christmas 1740 Robert Brisk, a labourer of Burstwick, was sentenced to be transported for seven years for stealing two rings.

In the early nineteenth century concern about the rising cost of poor relief nationally was to lead to reform of the old Elizabethan poor laws and the introduction of a much harsher regime of union workhouses. From 1837 Burstwick was one of the twenty-seven parishes in the Patrington Poor Law Union and housing paupers in the well-regulated workhouse there became the preferred way of discouraging all but the most desperate for applying for relief. To save money absent husbands were actively pursued when their abandoned wives and families became a burden on the poor rates. To this end on 1 June 1861 the clerk to the Patrington Union wrote to the overseers of the poor at Burstwick to say:

> I am directed by the Board of Guardians to request that you will take immediate steps to apprehend Robert Smith who has deserted his wife now in the Union Workhouse and chargeable to your parish.

By the second half of the nineteenth century Burstwick was less isolated than it had been earlier. In 1854 the Hull and Withernsea Railway opened and the station at Ryehill served the village.

Since the Second World War Burstwick has grown rapidly and by 2001 the parish population stood at 1813 having increased by around 800 people in just twenty years. One of its main features is that it became a very enterprising place with a number of businesses located there. One such enterprise is the design and manufacture of electronic components for the gaming industry. ECM Systems Ltd is based at Elifoot Park in the village and employs around fifty-six people in its factory and research department making bingo-related equipment for Mecca, Gala and other independent operators in the UK. The origins of the company however were far more humble for in the 1970s two Hull University laboratory

The Hare and Hounds is Burstwick's sole surviving public house/restaurant. In 1823 William Vickerman was the licensee.

Main Street, Burstwick, *c.* 1900 with a horse and carriage turning into Appleby Lane. *Image courtesy of Susan Hirst*

Main Street *c.* 1900 with the Hare and Hounds on the right. *Image courtesy of Susan Hirst*

Burstwick in the 1920s. Shown here is the Post Office on the corner of Pinfold Lane. Pensioners' bungalows now occupy the site. *Image courtesy of Susan Hirst*

An eighteenth-century cottage on Main Street. *Image courtesy of Susan Hirst*

technicians, Bill Neale and Robert Boothby, started the business in Bill's garage in Willow Road Burstwick. Their first project was to devise a rig for counting the number of bingo-players at an amusement arcade and from those beginnings the business began to grow.

In the twenty-first century, despite its rapid growth, Burstwick remains a village with a tremendous community spirit and this was shown by its response to the disastrous floods in June 2007. Although higher parts of Burstwick escaped unscathed around 120 houses on a new estate on the west side were badly affected and eight days of pumping were needed to dispose of the water. The residents mobilised to provide mutual aid in the aftermath of the disaster and this coming together resulted in the formation of Burstwick United a local flood action group. Led by chairman Ron Smith the group has campaigned vigorously for four years with the Environment Agency and others to make the village a safer place to live. In November 2011 Burstwick's new flood defences, cosing three million pounds, were officially opened.

CHAPTER 8

Elloughton

The expansion of villages to the west of Hull has been one of the most significant features of life in East Yorkshire in recent times and nowhere is this more apparent than in places like North Ferriby, Brough and Elloughton. In fact Elloughton became an increasingly popular place to live from the nineteenth century after the arrival of the railway at nearby Brough in July 1840. The attractiveness of the place soon began to attract newcomers able to commute by train and later by car into Hull and these days Elloughton-cum-Brough has taken on the dimensions and status of a town.

By studying old Ordnance Survey Maps, found on the East Riding Archives website, it becomes apparent how the open spaces between Elloughton and Brough

The serenity and beauty of Elloughton Dale to the north of the village is a paradise for walkers.

were soon filled with new development effectively merging the two communities. In 1823 the writer Edward Baines recorded that Elloughton and Brough had a combined population of just 383 people. By May 2011 Elloughton-cum-Brough had a population approaching 10,000 and in recognition of this growth the parish council became a town council.

While Elloughton may have grown since the beginning of the nineteenth century there is much to remind residents and visitors of the original character of the place. For those who enjoy exploring the picturesque locations of East Yorkshire Elloughton Dale, a wooded valley north of the village, cuts deeply into the chalk of the Wolds and has long been a popular route for walkers while at the heart of 'Old Elloughton' lies St Mary's Church dating from the thirteenth century. The origins of the place-name itself are obscure and may be linked with an Anglo-Saxon chieftain called *Aela* or derived from old-Scandinavian words meaning either 'hill with a heathen temple' or 'hill of a man called Helgi'. Whatever the truth of this Elloughton was important enough by the eleventh century to be mentioned in the Domesday Survey as 'Elgendon' and it was recorded that 'there was a priest and a church there'.

Until Elloughton became a favoured location of Hull's elite in the nineteenth century the village would have remained a small quiet place dominated by the needs of agriculture. In a directory of 1823 six farmers were named along with the usual trades of self-reliant communities of the time including two carpenters, two tailors, a blacksmith and a shoemaker. A flavour of life in rural Elloughton can be gleaned from the journals of one of its most illustrious citizens of the early nineteenth century, Barnabas Shaw: a pioneering missionary to South Africa. Shaw was born in the village on the 12 April 1788 and on a return visit to Elloughton in 1829 to see his aged parents wrote:

> The adjacent hills where I used to sit and play my flute while tending the lambs of the flock were clothed in living green; the fields I had frequently ploughed were waving with corn; and the beautiful Humber was rolling its mighty stream at the foot of the hills. What a contrast to the dreary deserts through which I had been travelling!

By 1891 the population had risen to 913 and a directory of the following year recorded that there were chapels belonging to the Congregationalists, Wesleyans, and Primitive Methodists as well as St Mary's Church (largely rebuilt in 1846). Anyone who has visited Elloughton Church will have seen a large brass memorial plaque in remembrance of four American naval officers who lost their lives during the *R38* airship disaster of 1921. The four had been living in Elloughton while the airship, bought by the US Navy, was undergoing trials at Howden. In October 1920 one of these officers, Flight Lieutenant Little, married his fiancée, Joy Bright, at St Mary's Church.

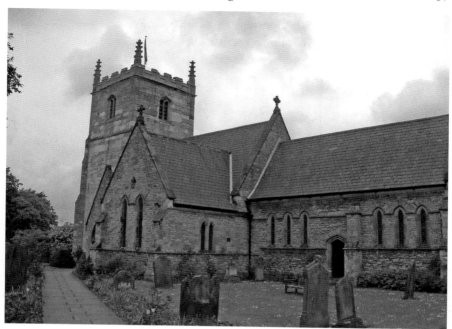

St Mary's Church at the heart of 'Old Elloughton' was built in the later thirteenth century and the tower was added in the early fourteenth century. There was major renovation in 1846. The church was badly damaged by fire in October 1964.

TO THE GLORY OF GOD
AND IN AFFECTIONATE REMEMBRANCE OF
COMMANDER L.H. MAXFIELD
L^T COMMANDER E.W. COIL
L^T COMMANDER V.N. BIEG
LIEUTENANT C.G. LITTLE
OFFICERS OF THE UNITED STATES NAVY
WHO GAVE THEIR LIVES IN THE DISASTER
TO THE AIR-SHIP R 38, 24TH AUG. 1921
IN THE SIGHT OF THE UNWISE THEY SEEMED TO DIE, AND THEIR DEPARTURE IS TAKEN
FOR MISERY AND THEIR GOING FROM US TO BE UTTER DESTRUCTION, BUT THEY ARE IN PEACE

The memorial plaque in St Mary's Church to the four Americans who had been living in Elloughton prior to the *R38* disaster. On the 9 October 1920 one of the United States naval officers in East Yorkshire, Flight Lieutenant C. G. Little married his American fiancée Joy Bright at St Mary's Church. He was killed in the disaster of the 24 August 1921 and is buried in Hull's Western Cemetery.

The *R38* airship was the largest of its day: 695 feet long and 122 feet in diameter with a gas capacity of 2,700,000 cubic feet. The design was a copy of the high-altitude wartime Zeppelins with a lightweight design that allowed a maximum performance to be achieved in thin air. Unfortunately no one had thought to calculate how it would handle in the denser air found at lower altitudes.

On Tuesday 23 August 1921 the airship carrying a crew of forty-nine (including seventeen Americans) set out from Howden on its fourth trial run. This took the *R38* down to Norfolk but by the next day it was back over the River Humber to undergo some low-altitude rudder tests; these were to simulate the kind of rough weather that might be expected over the Atlantic when the Americans were taking the ship home. In the event the tests proved too much for the fragile hull. At around 5.40 p.m. on the 24th witnesses standing on Hull Pier on the banks of the Humber and staring up at the silver cigar-shaped airship 2,500 feet above their heads reported seeing creases in its fabric. Within seconds the *R38* had broken in two and explosions swiftly followed as the hydrogen gas in the front section ignited. All forty-four members of the crew in that part of the airship were killed by a detonation of such intensity that windows over a large part of Hull's Old Town were shattered. The remains of the rear section however did not catch fire and plummeted into the River Humber.

With increasing car ownership in the inter-war years, for the wealthy at least, Elloughton continued to attract newcomers and one of these was Arthur Carmichael an optician and a co-founder of the famous department store: Carmichael's of Hull. In 1929 he bought Elloughton Garth a large house of sixteenth century origins together with three acres of gardens for the modest sum of £1,800. One of his children was the well-known actor Ian Carmichael (1920-2010) and in the book *Distant Days* (written by Elloughton resident Denny Lincoln) he gave some fascinating reminiscences of life in Elloughton in the 1930s. One feature of life there was the volume of traffic for Elloughton was on the main Liverpool-Leeds-Hull trunk road and, 'throughout the thirties traffic thundered through the village – lorries carrying timber and towing trailers loaded with huge bales of textile materials'. It was not until 1971 the Elloughton bypass was opened bringing an end to the traffic nightmare that had plagued the village.

The Carmichaels continued to live at Elloughton Garth until 1949 by which time their talented son Ian was well on the way to becoming an established actor. These abilities were shown well in a series of Boulting Brother's comedies like *Private's Progress* (1956) and he also starred alongside Peter Sellers in *I'm All Right Jack* (1959) a bitter satire about industrial relations of the time.

In the 1960s and 1970s Ian Carmichael developed a successful television career too, playing 'upper-class types' like Bertie Wooster in a BBC series based on the writings of P. G. Wodehouse and Lord Peter Wimsey in the mystery stories by Dorothy L. Sayers. His resilience as an actor was remarkable for at the age of eighty-three, long past normal retirement age, he was playing the part of hospital

Seven of the American crew of the *R38 en route* to Great Britain to train how to fly the airship. *Image courtesy of the Navy Historical Centre, Washington*

The maiden flight of airship *R38* on 25 June 1921. *Image courtesy of the Navy Historical Centre, Washington*

Above: The wreckage of the *R38* after it had broken up over the River Humber, exploded and crashed into the river. *Image courtesy of the Navy Historical Centre, Washington*

Left: Ian Carmichael's acting career spanned over sixty years from the Boulting Brothers film comedies of the 1950s to ITV's hospital drama *The Royal* in 2003 where he played the part of hospital secretary T. J. Middleditch. *Image courtesy of ITV Productions*

The Elloughton by-pass opened in 1971 and took heavy traffic away from the centre of the village.

secretary T. J. Middleditch in the ITV drama series *The Royal* set in his home county of Yorkshire.

Increasing car ownership and major improvements to the A63 since the Second World War has seen a rapid growth of new housing estates at Elloughton reflecting the appeal of the village as a very desirable place to live.

CHAPTER NINE

Rudston

Like many places in East Yorkshire the name Rudston seems to have come from the Anglo-Saxon invaders who arrived here after the departure of the Romans in the fifth century. However since the place-name is derived from 'rood-stone' it is clear that Rudston had long been a place of habitation and was probably a place of sun worship in Neolithic times, long before the building of the Christian Church of All Saints close by. The village is famous for the Rudston Monolith, standing twenty-six feet above ground level. This was probably erected around 1600 BC: the tallest megalith in the United Kingdom.

The monolith is composed of a type of stone found many miles away in the Cleveland Hills. We today can only marvel at the tenacity and skill of our ancestors

The Charioteer Mosaic from Rudston Roman Villa. *Image courtesy of Hull Museums*

in transporting the stone, said to weigh forty tons, to its prominent position on a spur of the Yorkshire Wolds, 125 feet above sea level. Excavations in the late eighteenth century suggest that there was as much stone below ground as is visible above it.

Apart from the Monolith there is a great deal of archaeological evidence to suggest that there was continuity of settlement at Rudston from pre-historic times. Neolithic and Bronze age barrows have been discovered as well as iron-age cemeteries in a valley north of the village. Another remarkable discovery was a Roman villa about half a mile south-west of the village. By the fourth century AD this contained the luxury features associated with Roman civilisation: mosaic floors, underfloor heating, wall decoration and a bath house. Excavations suggest that the villa was begun around the end of the first century AD (the earliest coin found has been dated to AD 81-96) on the site of an earlier iron-age farmstead. Archaeological investigation showed that Rudston had three ranges of buildings around a courtyard and that one of these was the bath suite. Bathing was a social occasion and bath suites contained a series of inter-linked rooms; at Rudston there was a warm room, a hot room and a cold plunge bath. The idea was to rub olive oil into the skin, get up a good sweat in the hot room and then to scrape off the oil and sweat using a curved instrument called a strigil. Participants would then take a refreshing dip in the cold plunge bath.

The bath suite at Rudston was equipped with under-floor heating where hot air from a furnace passed through the air space beneath the floor with gases and heat escaping through flues in the walls. Both the main living quarters and the bath suite of Rudston villa were equipped with mosaic floors indicating just how prosperous the estate was by the early fourth century AD. A mosaic floor of patterns or pictures was made of small cubes of coloured stone called tesserae. At Rudston, archaeologists found a storeroom with a large stock of ready-to-use and unfinished *tesserae*. The mosaic floors from Rudston (now to be found in Hull's Archeological Museum) are some interesting examples of the mosaic-builders art. The best of the mosaics, the Charioteer, was discovered in 1971 in what archaeologists believed was the main living quarters of the villa. This skillfully executed mosaic shows a Roman circus chariot with the charioteer holding a palm and a wreath (symbols of victory). In the four corners of the mosaic are designs representing the four seasons, a particular favourite of mosaic builders. The mosaics in the bath suite however seem to have been assembled later, possibly in the mid to late fourth century AD. By this time there may have been a growing shortage of skilled mosaic builders since the Venus Mosaic shows the figure of Venus with misshapen limbs. In comparison to the Charioteer Mosaic the Venus Mosaic is amateurish in design and may have been the work of a semi-skilled British craftsman.

The poor execution of the Venus Mosaic may be an indication of the problems facing the Roman Empire by the end of the fourth century AD. The economy of the Empire weakened due to a variety of factors including disease, the scarcity of

Left: The Rudston Monolith is a large standing stone dating to Neolithic times and was probably used in rituals involving the worship of the sun.

Above: The head of 'Spring' from the Rudston Charioteer Mosaic. *Image courtesy of Hull Museums*

Below: The Venus Mosaic from Rudston Roman Villa. *Image courtesy of Hull Museums*

slaves, the debasement of the coinage and increased taxation. The Empire was also racked by political instability and became increasingly unable to defend itself from the menace of barbarian tribes from outside. With the decline and eventual collapse of centralised Roman power, provinces such as Britain were left, by the end of the fourth century, to defend themselves against external attack. Without the support of a strong Roman army it seems that this was a challenge the local inhabitants were ill equipped to meet. Although lack of evidence means that we do not know when, precisely, Rudston Villa was abandoned the latest coin to come from excavations was a 'Constantine' from the late fourth century.

While in the centuries following the Roman occupation the ruling elite may have changed from Anglo-Saxon, to Dane and to Norman for the ordinary people of Rudston the care of the land and their animals remained of prime importance. By the time of the 1801 census the population of this lovely village standing on the banks of the Gypsey Race was 296 people. Many would have been employed as landless labourers by the ten farmers named in a directory of 1823. One of the main landowners was Godfrey Bosville who lived at nearby Thorpe Hall, a house of seventeenth century origins. The impact of this family on the locality can be seen at the Church of All Saints where there are several monuments to the Bosvilles while a directory of 1892 tells us:

> The church is lit by electricity conveyed by wires from Thorpe Hall, where there is a very complete apparatus of the most improved type. The cost, amounting to £430, was wholly defrayed by A. W. M. Bosville, Esq.

The directory of 1892 also gives us the names of the many tradesmen vital in such an isolated rural village and among these were James Burton (bootmaker), Walter Ferguson (tailor and draper) and John Watts (blacksmith and agricultural implement maker). Rudston was also noteworthy in having six carriers whose horse-drawn carts linked the village with important railway stations and market towns like Driffield and Bridlington.

Rudston is also famous for being the resting place of one of East Yorkshire's most celebrated writers, Winifred Holtby (1898-1935). The 1901 census shows that she lived at Rudston House and was the daughter of David Holtby, a prosperous local farmer. Winifred Holtby was educated at home by a governess before becoming a pupil at Queen Margaret's School in Scarborough and was a gifted child; her first significant work was a book of poems published when she was just thirteen. Later when she became an ardent feminist one of her role models was her mother Alice Holtby who was the first alderwoman on the East Riding County Council. In her famous novel, South Riding, she based the formidable figure of Alderman Mrs Beddows on her mother.

In 1917 Winifred Holtby enrolled as a student at Somerville College Oxford and although her degree course was interrupted by war service in France she graduated

Above left: The grave of Winifred Holtby in Rudston churchyard.

Above right: Winifred Holtby: writer, social campaigner and political activist was born in Rudston. *Image courtesy of the Hull History Centre*

A scene from the 1974 ITV production of South Riding. *Image courtesy of the ITV Picture Archive*

Thorpe Hall at Rudston.

and moved to London in 1921 with ambitions to become a writer. Although these days she is predominantly remembered as a novelist for books like *Anderby Wold* (1923), *The Crowded Street* (1924) and *The Land of Green Ginger* (1927) in her own lifetime she was seen more as a social rights campaigner, a journalist and a political activist. Having witnessed first-hand the terrible suffering of the First World War she was an ardent pacifist and in the 1920s travelled all over Europe lecturing for the League of Nations.

A prolific journalist, Holtby wrote for over twenty newspapers and magazines including the Manchester Guardian, the trade union magazine The Schoolmistress and the feminist journal Time and Tide. Ever more critical of the country's class system she began campaigning for the Labour Party but this was cut short in 1932 by ill health. Diagnosed with kidney disease she was told that she had only two years to live and devoted what remained of her life to her writing and to her most important novel South Riding. Winifred Holtby died in a London nursing home in September 1935 aged just thirty-seven.

At the time of the 2001 census Rudston parish had a population of 390 compared to around 550 a century earlier. With the Rudston Monolith to see and the grave of Winifred Holtby to visit Rudston attracts many visitors each year.

CHAPTER TEN

Preston

One of the interesting aspects of the history of the East Riding is the changing importance of places within the county. A thousand years ago neither Hedon nor Hull existed whereas at the time of the Domesday Survey in 1086 the village of Preston, (six miles east of Hull), an Anglo-Saxon settlement with a name derived from 'priest town', was already a place of significance. This great survey of England after the Norman Conquest showed that the township of Preston as well as having a church and a priest had eight manors and lords together with other vassals of the chief landowner of Holderness Drogo de la Beauvriere.

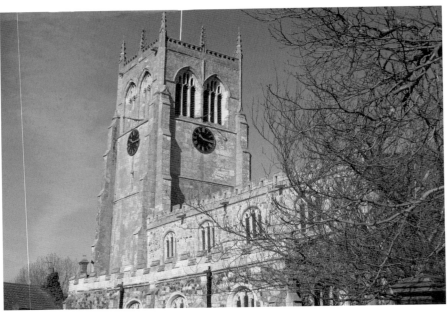

The magnificent church of All Saints at Preston. Parts of the nave date from the Norman or Early English period. There was much restoration in the late nineteenth century.

Anyone who has visited Preston will have seen its magnificent church of All Saints standing on higher ground at the centre of the village with the main street curving around the west end of the building. Parts of the church date from late Norman times and there were major restorations in the nineteenth century. Across the road from All Saints Church is a narrow path called Nuns Walk (part of the Preston Parish Trail) said to have been the route to a religious community founded in the Middle Ages under the patronage of Warter Priory.

During my visit to Preston I spoke to local expert Richard Thorp who has lived here for forty years. He told me:

In medieval times Preston had a navigable waterway from the Humber up to Neatmarsh Lane but this gradually silted up and became choked by weeds. Hedon was created, around 1140, from the Preston lands of the Count of Aumale because it had easier access to the Humber via Hedon Haven. When the same kind of silting happened there this led to the decline of Hedon as a port and to the growth of Hull.

Given the low-lying nature of South Holderness, less than seven metres above sea level, the land here was susceptible to flooding. The village of Preston stood a little higher and the number of roads radiating from it to Hedon, Bilton, Lelley, Burstwick and elsewhere indicates its importance as a 'focus'. In 1745 Preston became one of the places served when the road from Hull to Hedon via Bilton was taken over and improved by a turnpike trust.

Like most places in the East Riding farming would have been the main economic activity although there were the usual trades typical of any self-reliant village of the time. The large number of tradesmen here compared to other villages is an indication of how prosperous Preston had become by the early nineteenth century. A directory of 1823 recorded that Preston parish had a population of 828 people including thirty-one farmers and yeomen, five grocers, eight shoemakers, two blacksmiths, two corn millers, and three tailors. Census records help to give a human face to these statistics and that taken in 1861 provides details of those living on the Main Street. The Cock and Bell public house, still part of the village scene today, was in 1861 under the control of John Wallis, a seventy-four-year-old veterinary surgeon, while at the Blacksmith's Arms John Biglin, an agricultural labourer, was the innkeeper. Another census entry was for Hannah Fewster, a sixty-two-year old-widow who was described as 'sub-postmistress, grocer and wheelwright employing four men and one boy'. The trade of making and repairing wheels for horse-drawn carriages and wagons was already well established for a directory of 1823 said that David Fewster was the village wheelwright. Carrying on the family tradition was Hannah's son David (aged seventeen). Two other 'journeyman wheelwrights' and a fifteen-year-old apprentice were also part of the Fewster household of seven people.

The Nag's Head at the northern end of Preston opened in the 1870s. A directory of 1892 said that Thomas Clark worked there as an innkeeper and a joiner.

The giant petrochemical complex at Salt End on Preston's southern boundary. At the end of the nineteenth century the area was used for grazing, but in 1914 a tank farm was established there for the storage of petrol, oil and lubricants and a large wooden jetty was built into the Humber. BP has had a presence at Salt End since 1921.

For those who fell on hard times seeking help from the parish authorities and subsequent entry into the workhouse was often the last resort of the destitute. Feckless husbands and fathers became a target of the authorities when their families became a burden on the poor rates. One of these was John Petch of Preston, a blacksmith and innkeeper. Petch seemed to have a drink problem and in November 1858 he had been fined thirty shillings for keeping his public house in a disorderly manner. By 1861 Petch was described as a 'late innkeeper' and twice appeared before local magistrates for 'neglecting and refusing to maintain his wife and five children'. On the 18 February 1861 he had been committed to Beverley Gaol for a month after his wife and children had been forced, by the threat of his drunken violence, to flee from their home and seek shelter elsewhere. On the 15 April he again appeared before the magistrates since on his release from prison he 'had not endeavoured to support his family'. After pleading to be set free the JPs agreed to allow him two or three weeks to see if he would change his ways.

The parish of Preston covered an area of over 6,000 acres including a frontage on the River Humber at Salt End two-and-a-half miles away. In the days before the petrochemical industry dominated the skyline there Salt End was home to several cow keepers and dairymen. The availability of land and the proximity of Hull's population made this area, close to Hedon Road, suitable for some remarkable new developments from the late nineteenth century. Around 1887 a number of gentlemen formed a company that purchased around 260 acres of the Twyers Estate in order to establish a racecourse for Hull called Hedon Park even though it lay within Preston parish. The company built three stands and a clubhouse and since the Hull to Withernsea Railway lay close by a station was provided by the North Eastern Railway Company to serve race goers. The first meeting took place on 24 and 25 August 1888 with 14,000 people in attendance including members of the peerage like the Duke of Hamilton, the Duke of Clarence and Prince Albert Victor. Despite this auspicious start the new racecourse was never a financial success and meetings ceased in 1909. The blame for its failure was placed firmly on the shoulders of the railway company who it was said had never provided enough trains although stiff competition from other longer established Yorkshire racecourses like Beverley was probably a factor too.

Interestingly the demise of the racecourse coincided with the rise of the aviation industry and the one-mile straight next to Hedon Road was deemed suitable for pioneering aircraft to take off and land. In 1912 a young German, Gustav Hamel, arrived in Hull by train for the first flight over the city. Having assembled his Bleriot monoplane at the old racecourse the afternoon of 13 July 1912 saw him ready to make his pioneering attempt watched by excited spectators. As the *Daily Mail* reported:

The crowd was filled with doubts as to whether the airman would clear the rails in the distance but this fear was soon removed for he quickly reached a height of about 500 feet and sailed away amidst a storm of applause.

One of the distinctive features of Preston is the way its main street curves around the Church of All Saints.

Hedon Park Racecourse operated between 1888 and 1909 on the site of Twyers Farm. After the closure of the racecourse it was used for the pioneering flights of Gustav Hamel in July 1912.

Hull Corporation established a municipal airport on the site of the old racecourse in
1929.The most significant of its commercial flights was the weekly KLM service to
Amsterdam that began in 1934. Shown here are the passengers and crew in front of a
Fokker FX 11 aircraft. *Image courtesy of Hedon Museum*

The main street at Preston before the First World War. On the extreme right are the
premises of Thorntons: the village tailors. *Image courtesy of Paul Gibson*

An Air Pageant at Hedon Aerodrome in the 1930s. *Image courtesy of Hedon Museum*

Hamel's second flight lasted thirty-two minutes and took him over Hull, Hedon, Preston and Sutton before he returned to the racecourse. His third flight, following the railway line, towards Withernsea ended prematurely when he ran into a bank of low cloud two miles from the sea and decided to return.

Preston's early flirtation with flight was followed in the late 1920s by a decision of Hull Corporation to establish a municipal airport on the site of the old racecourse. The land was purchased for £17,400 and the new aerodrome opened on 29 October 1929 with 40,000 enthusiastic spectators in attendance.

With flying in its infancy Hull Corporation had some ambitious plans for their new airport. Perhaps of greatist significance for Hull's new airport was the decision of KLM in 1934 to begin a weekly service to Amsterdam. Yet the aerodrome was not without its critics and as early as October 1930 it emerged that the firm of British Industrial Solvents had been complaining to the Air Ministry in London about low flying over their factory at Salt End. In March 1935 one Hull councillor, G. K. Spruit went so far as to say that the location was unsuitable for an aerodrome and with Salt End's oil tanks close by it is easy to understand his reasoning on safety grounds alone. By 1939 Hull Corporation were considering plans for a new airport at the safer location of Neatmarsh Road, Preston but these schemes came to nothing for in the same month that work was due to start, September 1939, the Second World War began.

This put paid not only to Hull's new airport plans but also to the existing municipal airport.

The years after 1945 saw the increasing popularity of Preston as a commuter village and by 2001 the parish had a population of 3,100. Although rapid change has come to Preston in the last sixty years, the heart of the village would still be recognisable to the residents of a century ago. Yet though the Main Street is now much busier than it was Richard Thorp insists that Preston has the same 'sleepy and lethargic' atmosphere of days gone by. The place also retains a remarkable community spirit as shown by the village festivities in celebration of the Royal Wedding on 29 April 2011.

Easington

One of the most controversial subjects affecting East Yorkshire in recent times is how to deal with the threat posed by coastal erosion. For centuries the Holderness coast has seen its soft boulder-clay cliffs relentlessly eaten away by the power of the sea and it is estimated that in Roman times the coastline lay about two miles further east. A plaque in the centre of Easington, six miles south of Withernsea, records the 'disappearance' of fourteen nearby villages lost to the encroaching North Sea including Ravenser Odd (lost by 1360) and Dimlington (lost by 1850). Between 1851 and 1911 coastal erosion reduced the size of Easington Parish from 2,995 acres to 2,193 acres.

Easington's famous tithe barn with its thatched roof is unique in the East Riding and has timbers dated to the fourteenth century. During the 1920s it was used as an agricultural and folk museum. Its origins and past remain something of a mystery.

Like so many East Riding villages the name of 'Easington' come to us from Anglo-Saxon times and is thought to be derived from 'Esa's farm'. However archaeological evidence such as a Bronze Age burial mound and Roman pottery shows that there was settlement here much earlier. By the time of the Domesday Survey of 1086 the village was called Esingstone and it was recorded that Drogo de la Beauvriere was the chief landowner. In common with places elsewhere the oldest surviving building is the church standing on an elevated site at the heart of the village. Although the Church of All Saints dates from the twelfth century there is evidence that it replaced an earlier, Saxon, building. Another, unique, survival is Easington's famous tithe barn with a timber-frame and a thatched roof. The timbers used in its construction have been dated to the fourteenth century. In the Middle Ages these structures were commonplace across Yorkshire and were used to store the tithes (tenths) of produce given by tenant farmers to the parish priest. Another distinctive feature of Easington is the use of cobbles obtained from the seashore as a building material (as seen in the cobble wall around the churchyard).

Like most East Riding villages the economy of Easington would have been dominated by farming and other rural occupations under a communal system of open fields and commons until an Act of Parliament enclosed them in 1771. By the time of the 1821 census the population of the village was 488 people and in a directory of the time twelve farmers were named along with the usual trades of self-reliant communities of the time. By the time of the 1861 census Easington's population had grown to 600 while the 1881 census provides further details of them. Living at North Church Side was John Clubley, a sixty-two-year-old agricultural labourer, his wife Ellen a fifty-two-year-old dressmaker, his daughter and his son. At South Church Side lived John Quinton (age thirty-five) described as a grocer and draper, his wife and four sons.

By the 1850s fishing was a part of the Easington economy too perhaps stimulated by the arrival of the railway at nearby Patrington with the opening of the Hull and Holderness Railway in 1854. At the time of the 1851 census there were only two fishermen at Easington but by 1912 fishing employed eighteen men working thirteen boats. The 1901 census provides details of Easington's growing community of self-employed fishermen and living on Back Street in the village was Edward Curtis (age fifty-six) and his son William (age twenty-one). The census also shows that this fishing community came from a variety of places including Withernsea, Grimsby and Sheringham.

Easington's growing importance is perhaps also indicated by the fact that by the mid nineteenth century coastguards were to be found here too. As well as their duties in the prevention of smuggling the coastguards had a vital function in providing assistance to vessels in danger. They were supported by volunteers from Easington and elsewhere who operated life-saving apparatus (a rocket and breeches buoy) to rescue mariners in distress. During a great storm in March

Left: The church of All Saints was consecrated in 1190 and has a fairly unusual raised graveyard surrounding it. The church has three bells, one of which supposedly is from the lost village of Ravenser Odd, a village that used to be to the east of Spurn Point, but was destroyed by the sea in the late fourteenth century.

Below: Easington's beautiful community hall was paid for by the Norwegian energy company Gassco and opened in April 2006.

1883 the coastguard turned out with their rocket apparatus to rescue the crews of two Scarborough brigs that had come ashore near Kilnsea. From 1913 to 1933 their efforts were supplemented by an RNLI lifeboat called the *Docea Chapman* transferred from Withernsea. This carried a crew of thirteen men (ten of them oarsmen) drawn from the fishing community and a lifeboat shed was constructed in 1915. Despite the difficulties involved in launching and recovering the lifeboat from the beach twenty-eight lives were saved in nine successful rescues. One of these was on 25 January 1921 when a Dutch steam trawler came ashore and the Easington lifeboat rescued eleven of its crew. It was with great sadness that in May 1933 many Easington folk learned that their own lifeboat was to be replaced by a motor lifeboat based at Spurn.

It seems likely that Easington, despite its undoubted charms, would have remained a small, isolated, coastal village typical of Holderness had it not been for the fortuitous discoveries made in the 1960s off the coast. The opening of a huge new gas field in the Netherlands in 1959 sparked hopes among gas and oil exploration companies that the geology of the southern North Sea might yield similar results. In September 1965 the drilling barge *Sea-Gem* working for BP forty-two miles east of the Humber discovered significant quantities of gas beneath the seabed. In the House of Commons it was announced that the well was yielding ten million cubic feet of gas per day and that an investment in pipelines to bring this gas to Britain was justified.

Conveniently located to exploit the gas of the West Sole Field the BP Easington terminal opened in March 1967, the first place in the UK where natural gas had come ashore. The terminal continued to grow as Britain's towns and cities were converted from 'town gas' (manufactured from coal) to natural gas. These days the Easington complex consists of four sites: two of them run by BP, one by Centrica and the other by the Norwegian company Gassco. Since 2006 Easington has taken on even greater significance with the completion of the Langeled Pipeline delivering gas from the Norwegian sector of the North Sea to the United Kingdom and capable of supplying 20 per cent of the country's needs.

Having major companies like these on the doorstep has been of great benefit to Easington itself for they have been very generous to the community over the years in giving financial support to village activities like the Gala held between 1972 and 1998 and in paying for the publication of a village calendar since 2011. Even more impressive was the decision of Gassco to provide the money for Easington's new community hall opened in April 2006 and costing £650,000.

Above: The Marquis of Granby public house at Easington. In a directory of 1823 it was called the Granby's Head and Francis Walker was named as the licensee.

Left: The Easington Langeled Gas Terminal. *Image courtesy of Gassco*

Charles Medforth, the Easington shoemaker *c.* 1900. *Image courtesy of Mike Welton / SKEALS*

A painting by Alf Duck of the Easington lifeboat being recovered from the beach. *Image courtesy of Mike Welton / SKEALS*

1914

The Easington lifeboat crew in 1914. *Image courtesy of Mike Welton / SKEALS*

The blacksmith's workshop at Easington *c.* 1900. *Image courtesy of Mike Welton / SKEALS*

Overton Hall built in the seventeenth century was once one of Easington's most important landmarks. *Image courtesy of Mike Welton / SKEALS*

The Easington 'Pram Push' of 1968. *Image courtesy of Mike Welton / SKEALS*

CHAPTER TWELVE

South Dalton

The pretty estate village of South Dalton lies five miles northwest of Beverley. Largely owned by the Hotham family and closely linked with the nearby village of Holme-on-the Wolds this unspoilt and sparsely built community with its neat rows of cottages and Tudor-style houses has changed little in over a century.

One of the most impressive sights of South Dalton is the spire of St Mary's Church over 200 feet tall. This famous South Dalton landmark, paid for by Lord Beaumont Hotham, was a replacement for an older dilapidated structure demolished in 1860. The new church was designed by John Loughborough Pearson and built between 1858-1861 to serve both South Dalton and Holme on the Wolds.

The village pond at South Dalton on a Spring day.

Inside the church are a number of fine monuments to members of the Hotham family who have dominated this part of East Yorkshire for centuries. Probably the most famous of these is a black and white marble monument of Sir John Hotham, the second Baronet (1632-1689) and MP for Beverley in the late seventeenth century. The monument, said to have been made in Italy, represents him in life as a reclining knight in full armour and in death as a skeleton.

The Hotham family lived at nearby Scorborough until their house there burned down in 1705. They then moved to South Dalton where they inherited a late seventeenth century house on the site of the later Dalton Hall (built 1771-1776). By 1870 the Hothams owned ninety-seven per cent of the village of South Dalton and over 18,000 acres of land in East Yorkshire. These days the Dalton Estate is still run from offices in the village and employ joiners, plumbers, gamekeepers and others to maintain its stock of houses for rent, to supply timber, to provide support for its shooting parties and for its other commercial activities.

South Dalton lies on the lower slopes of the Yorkshire Wolds and seems to have begun life in Anglo-Saxon times with the name being derived from 'valley farm'. By the seventeenth century open fields lay all around the village with the common pastures occupying the high wold land in the west. The landscape here was greatly changed after enclosure by the creation of parkland surrounding Dalton Hall for this occupied about a quarter of the parish. As progressive landowners the Hothams invested considerable sums in both their estates and the village for after 1876 South Dalton had its own gasworks and waterworks. Other aspects of their forward-thinking generosity were the provision of a school in 1848, the erection of four cottages as almshouses for the poor in 1873 and the building of a reading room/billiard room in 1895. The latter was extended in 1927 and is now Dalton Holme Parish Hall and is well used for activities like the playgroup and the cricket club.

By 1851 the population of South Dalton stood at 299 and trade directories and census returns show the kind of trades and occupations typical of a farming village of the nineteenth century. Among the entries in the 1871 census, for example, is that of John Heward (age fifty-two) a 'farmer of four thousand acres employing four labourers and four boys', while at the shoemaker's shop lived Joseph Patrick (age sixty-two), his wife, his son and his fifteen-year old apprentice. The census also shows the presence of a tailor, a blacksmith, a carpenter and a grocer while agricultural labourers occupied several cottages.

In 1871 another cottage near the church was the home of Joseph Butler (age forty), a gardener employed at South Dalton Rectory, his wife Elizabeth (age thirty-nine) and his sons John Edward Butler (age six) and George Henry Butler (age one). In February 1880 both the family and the village became the centre of media attention when Elizabeth Butler murdered her youngest son and then tried to commit suicide herself. A neighbour had found ten-year-old George Butler 'screaming in great agony, his whole body contorted and his face discoloured' and

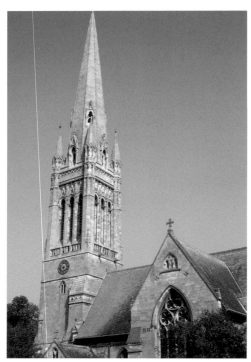

Left: The Church of St Mary has a spire 200 feet high. It was built between 1858-1861 to serve both South Dalton and Holme on the Wolds.

Below: The monument to Sir John Hotham the second Baronet (1632-1689). *Image courtesy of Austen Redman*

he died half an hour later 'before medical advice could be obtained'. Meanwhile Joseph Butler had discovered his wife 'in the pigsty in the garden with her throat bleeding'. Still alive but in a 'precarious state' she told a neighbour that she felt so wretched that she wanted to die but could not bear to leave her youngest son motherless. A local newspaper of 21 February 1880 reported that:

> The unfortunate woman, the author of the crime, has always borne an excellent character although of late she has shown symptoms of insanity.

At the subsequent coroner's inquest it was shown that the death of the ten-year old boy was the result of poisoning by vermin killer containing strychnine and administered by mixing it with gooseberry jam. The jury expressed the opinion that the 'mother was not of sound mind at the time' but at a court appearance in Beverley she was charged with 'wilfully murdering her son on the 12 February' and then remanded to Hull Gaol.

Although murder was a hanging offence in the nineteenth century it seems that Elizabeth Butler's mental state was a mitigating factor in the crime and she was declared 'not guilty by reason of insanity'. By the time of the 1881 census she was an inmate of Broadmoor Criminal Lunatic Asylum in Berkshire (opened in 1863) but did not remain there for the rest of her life. The 1901 census shows that Elizabeth Butler (now aged sixty-nine) had been freed and was living with her other son (John Edward Butler) at Temple Newsham near Leeds.

Old newspapers can often provide evidence of the dramatic occurrences in the life of a village but for more everyday matters school logbooks can be a useful source too. The logbooks of Dalton Holme Church of England School survive in the East Riding Archive in Beverley and provide a 'snapshot in time' of health problems typical of the days before universal health care and decent sanitation. An entry of 1880 for example reported: 'there is an offensive smell in the offices (toilets) coming from the cesspool at the rear of the school', while another of 1916 reported that the school nurse from Beverley had found that the heads of four girl pupils 'were in a very dirty and verminous condition'.

The Dalton Holme School Logbook also includes details relating to the impact of the First World War on the locality. An entry from 9 August 1916 recorded that:

> An aeroplane came down last night in a field about half a mile from the village. The children took to the fields and are now engaged in writing an account of their impressions.

In November 1917 the school was honoured by a visit from a war hero, Private George Chafer of the Yorkshire Regiment, who had won a Victoria Cross for his bravery during the Battle of the Somme. The logbook entry of 27 November records:

A lovely eighteenth century whitewashed cottage at West End in the village. A date plaque shows it was built in 1706.

A terrace of whitewashed cottages on the Main Street.

The Pipe and Glass Inn, West End, South Dalton is a public house/restaurant of national repute. In November 2011 it won the prestigious 'Michelin Guide Pub of the Year 2012' award.

The junction of the Main Street/West End on a Spring day.

Private GEORGE W. CHAFER. V.C

Private George Chafer (1894-1966) was a twenty-two-year-old soldier in the 1st battalion of the East Yorkshire Regiment. He was awarded the Victoria Cross for his gallantry in June 1916 when although severely wounded and under heavy enemy fire he succeeded in delivering an important dispatch to his commanding officer.

The Rector who introduced him gave the children a graphic account of what the brave soldier had done to obtain the coveted distinction. The Victoria Cross was shown to the children who then gave the hero three hearty cheers.

The logbook also shows that at a time of food rationing the school did its part for the war effort. On 9 March 1918 during National Egg Collection Week the children had collected sixty-eight eggs and sent them to the wounded at Beverley military hospital. In the 1920s and 1930s the County Inspector, Mr J. Moffat, frequently visited the school and made comments in his usual blunt manner on both pupils and teachers. In March 1922 he said:

> Miss Atkinson does not give the impression of being a strong headmistress. Discipline is weak – the children of the district appear to be uncommonly rough in their manner.

In the same report Moffat also revealed that the new infant teacher had annoyed some of the villagers by her attitude towards them. He wrote:

> Coming from the town into the country she has, I understand, given offence by a manner suggesting that the natives are so many uncivilised and inferior beings. The older children appear to have shown their resentment by being rude to her and she has retaliated on one or two occasions by boxing their ears.

South Dalton's school closed in 1966 with pupils being transferred to nearby Cherry Burton. Unlike many East Riding settlements the population of South Dalton has actually fallen in the last hundred years for in 1901 Dalton Holme parish had 264 people living there but by 2001 this had dropped to 197. Strict planning controls aim to keep the unique character of the place and this makes it appear that South Dalton is a village where time stood still.

CHAPTER 13

North Frodingham

Throughout the East Riding it is the church that usually provides the hub of a village community. However there are exceptions where villages have moved from their original location leaving the church isolated at some distance away. Brantingham and North Frodingham are good examples of this for at the latter the church of St Elgin lies about a quarter of a mile from the present day-village. Archaeological discoveries such as pottery, knives and a comb dating from the seventh to the ninth century AD suggest the area close to the church was the original site of the village of North Frodingham (six miles southeast of Driffield). Near to the church is Frodingham Beck (a tributary of the River Hull): an ideal

The Church of St Elgin. Parts of the church date from the twelfth century. The north aisle was added in the fourteeth century and the tower in the fifteenth century. The church was much decayed by the mid nineteenth century, but was restored in stages 1877-1891 thanks to the generosity of Sir Tatton Sykes, the fifth baronet of Sledmere.

landing place for the Anglo-Saxon invaders who began arriving from the fifth century. It is thought that it was the leader of one of these tribes, Froda, who gave the village its name.

In the *Domesday Book* of 1086 it was recorded that North Frodingham had both a church and a priest inferring that it was a place of some importance. In the Middle Ages communication by river and road made its location suitable as a meeting place for the buyers and sellers of foodstuffs and other products and so it became a market town. An indication of those prosperous times was the medieval market-cross that stood at the heart of the village and the original base of this survives. By the mid eighteenth century the weekly market had moved to Driffield but twice yearly fairs were still held until around 1900.

The village also benefited from the improvements made to the River Hull and Frodingham Beck by the promoters of the Driffield Navigation from 1767 and a new wharf and swing-bridge were constructed in 1825-6. The area around these became a hub of enterprise with, for example, the Frodingham Bridge Brewery shown on the 1855 Ordnance Survey map while a directory of 1892 said: 'The vessels anchor near the bridge, where there are warehouses and coal yards for the storage of the cargoes'. At the time of the 1901 census one of these vessels was a keel captained by George Porter from Beverley. The presence of ships' crews unloading cargoes at the wharf would also have brought trade to the Gate Inn nearby and to other North Frodingham public houses. A local newspaper reported, in November 1884, on the case of Robert Wray, keelman, who was arrested at the Star Inn for being drunk and disorderly. He was fined fourteen shillings by local magistrates.

Frodingham Landing remained in use until around 1960 to deliver coal for in the absence of a rail link water-borne transport remained the best way of transporting bulky goods. Curiously a map at Beverley Railway Station from around 1900 purports to show that North Frodingham was the terminus of a twelve-mile branch line linking the village, via Brandesburton and Tickton, with Beverley. In fact this North Holderness Light Railway remained stubbornly on the drawing board for in December 1901, before any work began, the North Eastern Railway cancelled the whole project. The company probably realised that the revenue generated by such a railway would not justify the cost of building it. Instead the villagers had to make do with a motorbus service that commenced in September 1903.

By the mid-nineteenth century the population of North Frodingham had grown to over 800 people and trade directories and census returns provide a valuable insight into how they earned their living. A directory of 1857 recorded the names of fifteen farmers while census returns from the same period show the presence of a large number of agricultural labourers living in properties on the village main street. One of these labourers was John Carr and on 2 December 1843 his wife Mary gave birth to a daughter: Rosalind. Better known as Rose Carr she was to become one of the most interesting characters of Victorian Holderness.

In the Middle Ages North Frodinghham was a market town. The market was probably held near to this medieval stone cross. The base is original but navvies allegedly destroyed the original cross *c.* 1800.

North Frodingham Bridge *c.* 1912 with the Gate Inn on the other side of the beck. The commissioners of the Driffield Navigation constructed the swing bridge and the quay *c.* 1825-1826 as part of improvements to Frodingham Beck. *Image courtesy of www.paul-gibson.com*

Although the later nineteenth century was the 'railway age' horse-drawn transport was still important for villages like North Frodingham not on the rail network. Directories of the East Riding contain the names of many people who served as carriers of goods. Rose Carr, skilled in the control of horses, became one of these and by 1866 was working as a carrier in the Driffield area.

In 1872 this tough and feisty woman, weighing nineteen stones and with a reputation for 'cracking heads together', bought and developed a business in Hornsea as a livery stable owner, as a carrier and as a cab and carriage proprietor. Rose and her horse-drawn cart became a familiar sight in the East Riding and she was said to be immensely strong; it was claimed that that she could carry a sixteen-stone sack of corn under each arm. By the turn of the century she had become a well-known figure at Hornsea Railway Station where she waited with other drivers for customers arriving on the Hull train. She also developed an amazing reputation as a hell-fire preacher at Methodist chapels across the East Riding from Preston to Brandesburton. By the time of her death in 1913 this remarkable businesswoman had developed an enterprise that hired out a range of horse-drawn vehicles including a hearse and employing three cabmen. Her estate was valued at over £1,400 – a considerable sum when the average wage was less than one pound a week.

Anyone who visits North Frodingham today will see its war memorial occupying a prominent position on the Main Street and commemorating the villagers who died during the First World War and to a lesser extent in the Second World War. For anyone who wants to carry out research on the impact of war on East Yorkshire villages it is possible to find out more about those whose names are recorded on war memorials by using the database on the East Yorkshire Regiment website (www.east-yorkshire-regiment.co.uk). On the North Frodingham memorial the name 'Tomlinson' figures prominently and in the East Riding Archive in Beverley a remarkable collection of letters survives to tell us more. The letters were written by Thomas Tomlinson and his brother Frederick on active service in France to their sister Doris back in East Yorkshire and reflect the nightmare world of trench warfare on the Western Front. Here death was a daily occurrence as soldiers launched fruitless attacks across no man's land in the face of withering machine-gun fire.

Frederick was a waggoner and a member of the 11th Battalion of the East Yorkshire Regiment. On 30 October 1917 he wrote:

It is awfully cold now and I think winter has set in. The blessed war is still going on but I don't think it will last much longer. I think he will soon have to give in as we have him absolutely beat.

Frederick's optimism was probably for his sister's benefit for their brother Thomas Tomlinson, serving with the 4th Battalion of the East Yorkshire Regiment, had

This map of the North Eastern Railway was added to Beverley Railway Station *c.* 1900. It shows the line from Beverley to North Frodingham as an accomplished fact. However the railway was never built because the NER cancelled the project in December 1901 on the grounds of cost.

Rose Carr, carrier, was born in North Frodingham in 1843 and became a familiar figure around the roads of Holderness with her horse and cart.

The War Memorial on Main Street commemorates those from the village who lost their lives in the First World War and the Second World War.

North Frodingham Windmill stood on the southwestern edge of the village. In an 1892 directory Moses Copeland was described as both farmer and miller. The mill ceased to operate around 1915 and was later demolished. *Image courtesy of the East Riding Museums Service*

The shop of R. E. Copeland (grocer and draper) *c.* 1910. *Image courtesy of the East Riding Museums Service*

A British trench during the Battle of the Somme 1916.

been killed during the Battle of the Somme in November 1916. On 16 November 1917 Frederick wrote to his sister:

It is just about a year ago now since he met his fate poor dear lad.

Frederick himself did not live to see the end of the conflict being killed on 25 March 1918 during the final German offensive of the war.

At the beginning of the twentieth century the population of North Frodingham stood at 555 people but by the time of the 2001 census it had grown to 712. While there has been some new house building in places like Manor Green and Low Farm Close the historic heart of North Frodingham, with its lovely Georgian farmhouses, has been protected by the creation of a conservation area in 2009. In the last fifty years North Frodingham has seen tremendous change with the loss of six farms (all dairy and pig farms), of three shops and a public house. Yet it still retains a tremendous sense of identity and community and attracts newcomers who wanted to enjoy a rural lifestyle while commuting to places like Driffield, Beverley and Hull.

CHAPTER FOURTEEN

Wawne

The village of Wawne, four miles south-east of Beverley was once an important crossing place on the River Hull. Since the 1960s the growth of suburban Hull and the creation of the Bransholme and Kingswood estates has filled the open farmland that once separated the village from nearby Sutton.

The name Wawne, or its alternative of *Waghen*, comes to us from the Anglo-Saxon period and is derived from 'quagmire'. As late as the mid seventeenth century it was reported that almost half of the area around the village was 'oppressed with water'. Yet there were some higher tracts of land and archaeological discoveries show that there was settlement here from prehistoric times; there is evidence of

Wawne Ferry *c.* 1910. In the small passenger boat is the ferryman Donald Brewer. In his hand he holds the 'stour' used to propel the boat across the River Hull by pushing it against the riverbed. In the background is the Windham Arms public house. Wawne Ferry closed in August 1946 and the public house in March 1967.

flint-working near the village dating to 4000 BC. In 1960-1962 excavations by the head-teacher and pupils of the local primary school unearthed pottery and other artefacts and reveal how Wawne was a thriving village in medieval times. This prosperity owed much to the patronage of the nearby Abbey of Meaux founded in 1150 by William le Gros, Lord of Holderness as a penance for failing to go on a pilgrimage to the Holy Land. By the thirteenth century the Cistercians at Meaux were taking part in the wool trade on a grand scale and their flocks of 11,000 sheep helped to supply the spinners and weavers of nearby Beverley.

As well as bequeathing land to the abbey William le Gros, around AD 1150, gave the monks a 'passage over the River Hull' and Wawne Ferry was to remain in their possession until the dissolution of the monasteries during the reign of Henry the Eighth. The ferry crossed the river from Wawne to Thearne at the site of an ancient ford and by the mid seventeenth century was owned by the Ashe-Windham family. From records in the East Riding Archive in Beverley we know of some of the expenses they incurred in operating the ferry. In January 1780 for example the ferryboat sank and twelve shillings was spent raising it from the bottom of the river. Soon after this incident a shipbuilder called William Wiseman from Lime Street in Hull was paid £60 to build a new ferryboat. The first launching of the new ferry in July 1780 was the cause of some celebration for we are told that eight shillings was spent on ale that day and a further 4s 6d on ale in November 1780 when 'taking the old ferryboat to pieces'. Another expense was the building of the Wawne Passage House (1783) and the premises later became a public house called the Anchor Inn operated by the ferryman.

From nineteenth century trade directories and census returns we can learn about those operating the ferry. By 1879 the landlord of the Anchor Inn and ferryman was James Brewer described in the 1881 census as 'a farmer of thirty-three acres employing three boys'. One of his sons, Donald Brewer, was later to become the ferryman himself and in 1911 he bought the ferry rights, the public house (renamed the Windham Arms) and the farm for £2,100 when the Windham Estate was sold at auction. Sales particulars from the time showed that the income from the ferry averaged about £52 per year.

Travelling on Wawne Ferry could be a hazardous business for both the ferryman and his passengers. As Jack Clarkson, who worked for Donald Brewer in the 1930s, said:

> It was a work of art taking the ferry across the forty-five feet of water which lay between one bank and the other. If the wind and tide were going the same way it could be difficult to get across.

From local newspapers it is possible to learn of these difficulties and the *Hull Packet* reported on the issues encountered by the Holderness Hunt in using the ferry. In February 1867 the newspaper said that 'the hounds were late coming in

The pontoon ferry or floating bridge being used to transport the horses and hounds of the Holderness Hunt across the river. The ferryman pulled the pontoon ferry across the river using chains fastened to the river banks.

Wawne Hall was the home of the Windham Family, important local landowners. It was demolished in the 1950s to make way for new housing. *Image courtesy of the Sutton Resource Centre*

as the ferry-boat at Wawne had been swamped in the night and was lying at the bottom of the river so they had to go round, five or six miles, by Hull Bridge'. There were further problems in December 1895 when it was reported that when the pack arrived at the Thearne side a storm had made the river 'like a sea' and it was difficult for both hounds and huntsmen to get across.

Successive generations of ferrymen learned how to judge the river conditions to propel the small passenger boat across using a 'stour' or pole about eight feet long. Until around 1884 this operation was straightforward since the river at this point was relatively shallow because of the existence of the Wawne Ferry Ridge (the site of the earlier ford). However the dredging of the river led to complaints from the Windhams in October 1885 that the operation of the ferryboat and the use of the landing stages had become more difficult. Compensation from the river authorities led to the purchase of a pontoon or floating bridge ferry pulled by chains across the river and used to transport horses, vehicles and agricultural machinery. The pontoon was useful at high tide too since the stour used to propel the ferryboat would not reach the bottom of the river at these times. Yet even with the pontoon there could be mishaps and on 10 June 1899 a local newspaper reported on a serious accident to a horse and trap *en route* from Beverley to Sutton.

It appears that in descending the slope to the ferry the horse was unable to hold properly in check the conveyance with the result that its missed its footing on the boat, swerved and fell headlong into the river. The horse dragged after it the trap and two of its occupants who were immersed in the deep water but who luckily escaped without receiving any further harm. The horse however was drowned before it could be rescued.

By the 1920s Donald Brewer was charging foot passengers one old penny, cyclists two old pence and the owners of small cars six old pence to use the ferry. An RAC handbook of the time shows that the service operated on demand seven days a week from 6 a.m. to 10 p.m. Those arriving at the Thearne side of the river had to shout 'boat!' to get his attention. An observer from a local newspaper in June 1922 was clearly impressed with how busy the ferry could be for he wrote:

The other evening inside an hour the traffic taken across included a large four-seat car, a motor cycle and sidecar, a racehorse, a pony and trap and any number of cyclists.

As long as the number of bridges remained limited the ferry provided a valuable service but as the city of Hull began to expand from the beginning of the nineteenth century so did the number of bridges across the River Hull. One of these was Sutton Road Bridge built in the late 1930s and less than three miles downstream from Wawne. The opening of this bridge is likely to have had an adverse effect on

A horse and trap on Wawne's very muddy main street *c.* 1900. *Image courtesy of the Sutton Resource Centre*

Joiner's shop and blacksmiths *c.* 1900. George Westerdale Blakey, the joiner, is on the right. *Image courtesy of the Sutton Resource Centre*

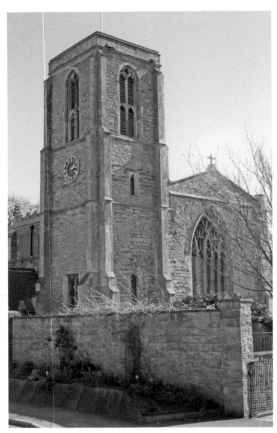

Left: The Church of St Peter at Wawne. The first known reference to a church at Wawne was in AD 1115.

Below: Wawne Church *c.* 1910 *Image courtesy of the Sutton Resource Centre*

Above: Bob and Eliza Wray of Prospect Farm Thearne being transported across the River Hull in the 1930s.

Right: Wawne Ferry after closure *c.* 1950. The pontoon ferry lies abandoned and derelict on the river bank.

The Waggoners public house at Wawne was opened in the 1970s.

the use of the pontoon ferry by motor vehicles though local farmers continued to use it to move agricultural machinery.

Wawne Ferry remained in operation during the Second World War but in May 1944 the elderly Donald Brewer passed control of the Windham Arms and the ferry to his nephew Harold Walker. After only two years Walker decided to sell both. On 19 August 1946 he finalised the sale of the Windham Arms, the farm and the ferry rights to Moors' and Robson's Brewery in Hull for £3,000.

We know that late August 1946 marked the end of the 800-year-old-ferry because within weeks a local politician had contacted the brewery to ask why it had stopped running. He was told that that the ferryboat was no longer safe to use and that the cost of repairing or replacing it was not justified by the income from people using it. During 1947 the issue of Wawne Ferry was investigated thoroughly by East Riding County Council and they believed that the brewery had a duty to 'carry all wayfarers across the river'. Yet in reply to their demands that the ferry should reopen the brewery responded by saying that 'no obligation rested on themselves or their tenant to maintain the ferry'. In the event however the County Council were not prepared to pursue the matter through the courts since the legal position on whether Wawne Ferry was a public ferry or a private one was unclear.

At the time of the 1891 census Wawne had a population of 393 people but by 2001 this had grown to 878 reflecting the appeal of the village as a commuter settlement for Hull and Beverley. There was a considerable expansion of private housing along Meaux Lane and Greens Lane while the demolition of Wawne Hall allowed for the creation of more houses in Windham Crescent.During the Second World War Wawne Hall had been the headquarters of the anti-aircraft batteries north of the Humber and after 1945 part of the site was retained for emergency planning and civil defence. By 1949 the increasing tensions of the Cold War and the danger that this might escalate into a conflict using weapons of mass destruction led to the choice of the Wawne site for a nuclear bunker. Protected by blast doors the bunker once housed a number of underground rooms for the fire service, for radio and telephone communications, for operations like plotting the patterns of nuclear fallout and for a Radio Humberside studio that could be used to broadcast instructions to any survivors.

With its thriving community spirit and its tranquil environment it is not surprising that Wawne continues to attract people who want to live close to the city but to be near to the countryside.

CHAPTER FIFTEEN

Seaton Ross

One of the effects of the disastrous floods of June 2007 was to show how the landscape of the East Riding could be altered by high rainfall. Low-lying areas were quickly turned into lakes. Yet three centuries ago when drainage methods were far more rudimentary than they are today large parts of East Yorkshire lay under water including the Hull Valley and parts of Holderness. Place names can sometimes provide us with clues as to locations that were flooded and the name of Seaton Ross, six miles west of Market Weighton, is partly derived from the sea or marsh that once separated the village from nearby Holme on Spalding Moor while *ton* refers to a an enclosure or farmstead. The suffix 'Ros' was added in the

The Black Horse public house in Seaton Ross. In a directory of 1892 Christiana Walker was described as a beer retailer at the Black Horse.

sixteenth century when possession of the land came under the control of the de Ros family.

The village of Seaton was mentioned in the Domesday Book of 1086 when it was recorded that before the Norman Conquest 'Gamel son of Karli' was the lord of the manor and that there were ten villagers and one priest. Saxon rebellions against the Norman invaders led to the Harrying of the North by King William the First and the Domesday Survey recorded that the land around Seaton Ross was now 'waste'.

In the centuries that followed most of the inhabitants would have been engaged in farming or other rural occupations under a communal system of open fields and common pastures until these were enclosed by act of parliament in 1757. The Constable-Maxwell family of Everingham owned much of the land here and among their tenants was John Watson from a long established farming family. Watson had a large farm at Seaton Ross consisting, in 1798, of some 300 acres and his status is indicated that by the fact that he also acted as a churchwarden and a collector of the land tax. In 1777 he had married Sarah Wilberfoss and they went on to have eight sons and three daughters. Their fourth son, William, was born in May 1784 and he followed the family tradition for a directory of 1823 records that he was a 'collector of taxes' living at Seaton Lodge, a farm of 138 acres. William Watson (1784-1857) was a remarkable individual with a thirst for knowledge and self-improvement for his self-taught talents extended beyond farming to land surveying, map making and the construction of sundials. In the East Riding Archive in Beverley a collection of his work survives and among these is a scrapbook showing his surveys of Seaton Ross and preliminary sketches of sundial projects. In a book of verses from 1824 William Watson wrote:

I am a farmer, which I tell, I also know surveying well, dials I've made many sorts, at school I did not learn these arts.

Watson's interest in sundials may have arisen from simple curiosity or from an obsessive interest in timekeeping for it is recorded that he 'wanted to convey to his workers that punctuality mattered hugely, especially first thing in the morning when reporting for work'. Watson wrote a treatise on sundials in 1824 and among the early examples of his work is a small sundial above the south door of St Edmund's Church and dated 1825. Nearby an epitaph on his tombstone reads:

At this church I so often with pleasure did call,
That I made a sun dial upon the church wall.

Even more impressive are sundials that Watson completed around 1840 on Sundial Cottage at North End in Seaton Ross and at Dial Hall Farm. Twelve feet in diameter these sundials bear testament to Watson's skills as a mathematician,

Although there was probably a church on the site from early times the present church of St Edmund dates from 1789.

Sundial Cottage at North End, Seaton Ross

draughtsman and astronomer. For those who wanted them his sundials were available to order for Watson wrote:

> If any person wants a dial, apply to me I'll make a trial, I now can make for any man, upon a much improved plan, five guineas is the price of one and each mile distant half-a-crown.

Meanwhile Watson's abilities as a land surveyor enabled him to find work elsewhere. By 1845 he was living at Pocklington and he later moved to Market Weighton where he was described as a surveyor of roads. His most important works were illustrated plans of Market Weighton (1848) and Pocklington (1855). In the latter he used his skills as a draughtsman and mapmaker to combine details of what houses looked like with the names and professions of those living there. Watson died unmarried at Seaton Ross on 4 December 1857 leaving his estate to his brother James.

Census returns and trade directories reveal that Seaton Ross was a typical farming village in the nineteenth century with a population (in 1821) of 477 people. Fifteen farmers were named in a Seaton Ross directory of 1823 and among the other occupations listed were a carpenter, a butcher, a shoemaker and a tailor. Another essential trade for any self-reliant village was that of blacksmith and working at his forge in 1823 was William Pexton, the landlord of the Blacksmith's Arms Public House. Licensee's who allowed their customers to become too inebriated on their premises could face the full vigour of the law. From a local newspaper we learn that Robert Howden was the innkeeper of the Blacksmith's Arms in 1878 and in June of that year he was fined £1 plus costs for allowing James Leach of Hull, a farm baliff, to become drunk there. Life in this 'long and straggling village' (as it was described in a directory of 1892) changed little in the years that followed. At the time of the 1881 census one of those named was Stephen Walker (age thirty-five) a farmer of sixty acres employing one labourer and one boy while George Jackson (age forty-six) was described as a grocer and carrier, an essential service in a village where the nearest railway station was located at Holme-on-Spalding-Moor three miles away. In the later nineteenth century carriers also linked Seaton Ross with Market Weighton and York.

Another vital trade in the rural economy of the time was that of miller and the stump of the windmill tower at Old Mills in the village survives to remind us of the former importance of this occupation. Wind power could be unreliable at times and so in the 1850s the mill owner, Richard Hartley, added a steam-powered mill to enable production to continue throughout the year. The new engine shed with its seventy-foot chimney contained a twelve horsepower engine capable of carrying out an 'extensive and profitable business'. This continued until the growing importation of North American wheat made it more profitable to locate flour milling at major ports like Hull.

The stump of the windmill tower at Seaton Ross today.

Old Mills at Seaton Ross *c.* 1900 with the steam powered mill to the left of the windmill.

Above: The Silver Jubilee celebrations at Seaton Ross in 1977.

Right: The sundial above the church door was provided by William Watson in 1825.

Like many East Riding villages Seaton Ross has seen major changes since the Second World War with the disappearance of trades that were once commonplace and a decline in the numbers employed in farming. Yet the village retains a vibrant economy and one major success story has been St Helen's Farm which specialises in goat milk products.

By the time of the 2001 census Seaton Ross had a population of 545 people and one of its attractions is a long main street with older properties interspersed with new. It is a village that continues to attract newcomers and has a thriving community spirit as shown by the efforts made by villagers to celebrate the Queen's Diamond Jubilee in June 2012.

CHAPTER SIXTEEN
Millington

Although many locations in the East Riding can lay claim to being the prettiest in the county few can match the attractive setting of Millington, two miles north-east of Pocklington. As you wind your way from Huggate along the dry valley known as Millington Vale the local beauty spots of Millington Woods and Millington Pastures come into view and are truly breathtaking. The former, occupying Lily Dale, is one of the few remaining wooded dales in the Wolds and was declared a local nature reserve in 1991 because of its scientific importance. It has been described as the richest botanical woodland in the East Riding and its ash trees and rare species of plants and flowers (like its bluebells in Spring) provide an

The scenic beauty of Millington Pastures on a spring day.

enriching experience for all visitors. Millington village itself contains some lovely old cottages and farms sheltering under the steep slope of the Wolds. Like other places in East Yorkshire it was probably the ready availability of water from a spring that determined the location of the village.

While the name Millington comes to us from Anglo-Saxon times and is derived from 'farmstead with a mill' there was a settlement here much earlier. Earthworks in Millington Pastures date back to 2000 BC while other archaeological evidence suggests that Millington was a favoured location of Romano-Britons too. Excavations in 1745 by the York antiquarian Francis Drake and his companion Dr John Burton revealed what was believed to be a circular Roman temple, 45 feet in diameter together with the foundations of other buildings containing mosaic floors, tiles, coins and other artefacts. It was believed by those at the time that the remains of the temple and the foundations of a nearby house marked the site of the Roman settlement of Delgovicia although more recent investigations in 2002 cast doubt on this theory.

By the time of the Domesday Book (1086) Christianity had replaced the pagan beliefs of earlier times and Millington had its own church with Norman features (like its porch) still evident. Another aspect of Millington Church well worth seeing is the 'Leper's Window' said to have been placed in the south wall of the chancel so that those afflicted by this terrible disease could observe church services from outside and not alarm or infect the rest of the congregation. Millington may have been a small rural community but it was not without problems for documents in the East Riding Archive reveal that some inhabitants could be troublesome. A petition of the early eighteenth century made a complaint about James Bankus and his wife Frances and asked that the village constable should take them into custody. The petition alleged that the pair 'lived wicked and dissolute lives chiefly by begging and stealing and that they had desperately threatened to set fire to the houses and burn down the whole of Millington and that at such time of night that some of the inhabitants should not escape with their lives'.

Millington is a place best explored on foot and one important building to see is the Gait Inn dating back to the sixteenth century. The name refers to the 'gaits' or areas of land that each farmer had on Millington Pastures after the 'enclosure act' of 1768. A 'gait' was, for example, enough pasture to support six sheep and over 100 people once had these grazing rights. A further reminder of Millington's rich agrarian heritage is the 'hooping wheel' found on the main street and once used by blacksmiths and wheelwrights to shape the iron rims of cartwheels.

A directory of 1879 named Richard West as the village blacksmith and the 1881 census shows that he had been born in Barmby Moor. Living with the sixty-year-old Richard West in 1881 was his wife Rachel together with his daughter and granddaughter. The 1881 census shows us the names and occupations of a typical East Riding rural village. One of those in the census was John Jenkinson (aged thirty-six) a farmer of 160 acres employing one labourer and one boy. Living with

Parts of Millington church date from the eleventh century. The south door has a three-tier Norman arch while the tower, made of brick, was a more recent addition.

The Gait Inn at Millington dates back to the sixteenth century. In a directory of 1823 James Dales was named as the licensee.

Jenkinson was his wife and two children, Rachel Birks a fifteen- year-old domestic servant from Huggate and Simpson Clerk a sixteen-year-old farm servant from Barmby Moor. At the other end of the social scale elsewhere in the village was Thomas Stamp, a twenty-three year old farm servant, his wife Alice together with five daughters and one son. Census returns and trade directories show that Millington had the usual occupations of self-reliant communities of the time like a miller, a tailor and a carrier.

Another important figure was the schoolmaster and in 1881 this was Alfred Ottley from Arundel in Sussex. Assisting him in his teaching was his wife, Betsy Ann, who came from Pocklington. The school logbook survives in the East Riding Archive and reveals the same kind of 'funding issues' and attendance problems typical of rural schools. On 25 March 1874 the schoolmaster wrote:

I find a great many of the children without any slates which I think ought to be bought by the children themselves for their lessons.

On 7 May 1875 Alfred Ottley wrote, 'Only ten pupils at school this morning. Several children are tending cattle in the lanes' It was with growing frustration that Ottley wrote in May 1876:

Its of no use: we cannot get these children to attend. Something must be done in this place or no master can teach. One boy by the name of Wilson has only attended on thirteen days in thirteen weeks.

Some of the Millington School accounts also survive and those from 1879 show that the schoolmaster received an annual salary of £241 8s 9d and that the income of the school came from sources like 'school pence' paid by the pupils (£4), a church collection (£1 1s), endowments of £9 and £4 10s and subscriptions like that from St John's College Cambridge of £3 6s 8d. From the directory of 1879 we know that 'the Master, Fellows and Scholars of St John's College' were the lords of the manor here.

The school logbook continued to point to the difficulties and frustrations that the schoolmaster faced with attendance when local farmers regularly employed children at busy times of the year. A variety of other reasons were also put forward to explain absence and on 22 November 1907 he wrote:

Six boys played truant on Monday afternoon to see a fox hunt and four today to see a funeral.

Inspection reports from the 1920s reveal other weaknesses of Millington School even though in 1922 there were only twenty pupils. The East Riding Schools Inspector, Mr J. Moffat, was critical of the headmistress, Mrs Fairweather, claiming that her 'discipline could be more bracing'. In April 1922 he wrote:

The Rambler's Rest at Millington is a popular place of refreshment for weary cyclists and walkers.

Millington is a popular village for walkers and cyclists.

Millington Pastures is famous for its sheep and its Highland Cattle.

Millington in the 1930s.

A steep slope of the Yorkshire Wolds shelters Millington.

Fortunately for the school Mrs Fairweather may possibly retire before the age of sixty. With the exception of her kind and obliging manner she does not show many good points. Her appearance is rather untidy and her teaching is feeble and lacking in enthusiasm.

Unfortunately her replacement, Miss Meek, seemed to live up to her name for the inspector wrote, 'the children seem to please themselves as to whether they do any work'. By October 1924 he appeared to believe there were grounds for her dismissal claiming that she was 'markedly inefficient' but softened his criticisms by saying that she was, 'so simple, childish and helpless that I cannot help feeling sorry for her'.

From his reports it seems that even more robust teachers found Millington School a trial for in May 1933 the inspector wrote:

About six of the children are of the dull heavy type: slow mentally and difficult to teach.

By the 1920s Millington already had a reputation as a place to visit and an article in a local newspaper described the village as 'quaint' and a place of 'picturesque beauty' in the summer months. The same reporter referred to the rugged countryside of Millington Pastures as the 'Switzerland' of the area and said it was a rendezvous point for picnic parties and holiday campers.

Since the Second World War and the growth of walking as a pastime Millington has become even more popular for both the Minster Way and the Wolds Way long distance footpaths pass through or close by the village. Apart from being a magnet for walkers and cyclists Millington is a place with a thriving community spirit as shown by village celebrations for the Jubilee in June 2012. These included fireworks, the lighting of a beacon and the presentation of commemorative medals to village children.

CHAPTER 17

Eastrington

The expansion of villages to the west of Hull has been one of the most significant features of life in East Yorkshire since the Second World War and Eastrington, Gilberdyke and Newport are just some of the places that have seen an influx of newcomers. The improvement of the A63 trunk road and the completion of the M62 motorway in 1976 made long-distance commuting by car, to the east or the west, a more realistic prospect and helped to make these villages attractive places to live. Within easy distance of junction 37 of the M62 the growing popularity of Eastrington, three miles east of Howden, is indicated by the rise in its population.

St Michael's Church at Eastrington. Begun in Norman times the architectural features of the building seem to date it to the fourteenth century.

In 1891 the population of the village was 436 but by 1971 this had grown to around 600 while the 2001 census showed that it was now 880.

The appeal of the village was also helped by its access to the railway and Eastrington was one of the first villages to be served when the Hull and Selby line opened in 1840. In the early days of rail travel accidents were fairly commonplace and Eastrington Station was the scene of one such mishap. A local newspaper reported that on 1 March 1842 a squall of wind drove an empty coal wagon out of a siding onto the main line. There was then an accident when a train coming up behind the wagon collided with it and came off the rails. When the Hull and Barnsley Railway opened in 1885 villagers had the luxury of having two stations. In a directory of 1892 Thomas Atkinson was named as the stationmaster at the NER station while Fred Bamforth performed the same function at the rival Hull and Barnsley Railway Station. This situation continued until the Hull and Barnsley line closed to passengers in 1955 although coal trains continued to pass through until the early 1960s. These days the other Eastrington Station continues to serve the village with trains to Hull and York.

Like so many villages in East Yorkshire the origins of Eastrington can be traced back to Anglo Saxon times for the name is thought to be derived from ' a farmstead belonging to the people living to the east'. Until the land around the village was enclosed by act of parliament farming was undertaken under a communal system of open fields and commons. After the Norman Conquest of 1066 King William gave Howden Manor, of which Eastrington was a part, to the Bishop of Durham and it remained in the hands of the diocese for the next five hundred years.

In a simple agrarian village like Eastrington much depended on the work of unpaid officials chosen from the local community like the pinder who rounded up stray animals and the parish constable who arrested wrongdoers and brought them before local magistrates. Other parish officers were the overseers of the poor who levied a local rate or property tax on landowners for the support of paupers among the infirm, the elderly and unmarried mothers or made arrangements for the care of orphans. Those who neglected their duties could find themselves on the wrong side of the law and from Quarter Sessions records we know that in 1799 Thomas Claybourn, the village constable, was charged with 'negligently permitting the escape of John Arnold from his custody at South Cave while conveying him to the House of Correction at Beverley'. The criminal code of the time could be extremely harsh on those who broke the law especially those involved in 'public order' offences like riot. After the 'Militia Riots' of 1757 several Eastrington men were arrested including Henry Thomas, the village blacksmith. Another, Robert Nurse, was charged with high treason but died in prison at York in 1758 before he could be brought to trial.

Eastrington remains one of the best-documented villages in the East Riding thanks to the work of local historian Susan Butler whose detailed book on the history of the village was published in 2009. Susan told me:

The Black Swan public house at Eastrington. In a directory of 1892 Henry Jackson was the licensee.

The village hall and cricket ground at Eastrington.

I was brought up in Eastrington where my mother's family had lived since the seventeenth century. My village history took me around thirty years to research and write. The problem was that there was always something new to find out but I finally decided enough was enough and published.

Thanks to Susan's enthusiasm and hard work there is also a great deal to be learned about Eastrington from her 'Howdenshire History' website including the census returns from the village in 1851, 1891 and 1901. A study of the 1851 census shows that Eastrington was a typical farming village and there were many households where the main wage earners were agricultural labourers together with the usual trades and occupations of self-reliant communities of the time like a shoemaker, a wheelwright and a blacksmith.

The 1851 census also reveals the names of several 'paupers' dependent on the 'parish' for poor relief. Typical of their number was Agatha Ellis; in 1851 she was a forty-three-year-old widow and mother to three children. From 1837 Eastrington became one of the forty parishes of the Howden Poor Law Union and the guardian's minute books survive in the East Riding Archive in Beverley. In order to save money neglectful or absent parents were often pursued through the courts and on 7 December 1839 it was recorded that a 'warrant be obtained against Sarah Sanderson for neglecting to maintain Mary Ann Sanderson her illegitimate child now chargeable to Eastrington'. A year later the authorities were chasing James Marshall for the maintenance of a child he had fathered by Catherine Ward of Eastrington.

Increasingly care in a well-regulated workhouse became the preferred option of dealing with paupers and a new 'union workhouse' was built at Howden in 1839. One category of inmate was orphan children and the 1881 census shows the presence in the Howden workhouse of the Eastrington paupers Susan Pillock (age thirteen) and her brothers Herbert (age fourteen) and Henry (age eight). Destitution and admission to the workhouse were ever-present threats in the nineteenth century for even well to do families could fall on hard times. One of these was the Norwood family who were tenants of Townend Farm, one of the largest in the village. The death of William Norwood in December 1838 marked a change in the family fortunes for by 1851 they had given up the farm and William's eldest son was now in the workhouse and described as a 'pauper farm labourer'.

A village directory of 1892 shows that Eastrington was a typical agrarian-based village at that time with sixteen farmers supported by the usual range of tradespeople, shopkeepers, publicans and so on. Two blacksmiths were named in the directory and one of these, Joseph Driffill, was also the innkeeper of the Cross Keys Public House.

Since the Second World War many of Eastrington's former occupations like its blacksmith and saddler have disappeared but one interesting new business in the 1960s catered for the thriving hobby of 'stamp collecting' among the young. The

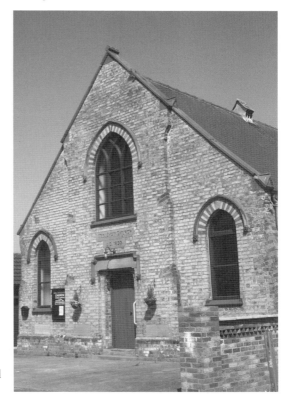

Right: Eastrington's Wesleyan church dates from 1893.

Below: Moss Farm on the High Street at Eastrington has an unusual chequered brick pattern.

Eastrington Station on the old Hull and Barnsley Railway. Fred Bamforth was the stationmaster here in 1892. Eastrington was unusual in that it had two railway stations until the Hull and Barnsley Railway closed to passengers in 1955.

The shop of Edmund Flint in the centre of Eastrington *c.* 1910. *Image courtesy of Susan Butler*

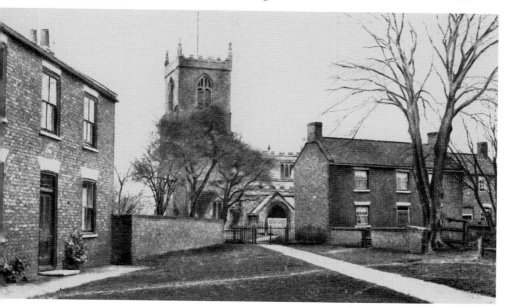

The village green at Eastrington *c.* 1910. *Image courtesy of Susan Butler*

'philatelic business' of Dennis Hanson based in Eastrington sent packs of stamps 'on approval' by post to customers all over the UK and employed many local people.

In the twenty-first century Eastrington has a shop, a public house and a garage while farming retains a presence. Despite the residential growth of the village it has also kept a thriving sense of community and the village hall, built thirty years ago, is well used for activities like cricket, badminton, zumba dancing, bowls, a pre-school group, keep fit and flower arranging.

CHAPTER 18

Kirkburn

In recent years tranquillity has been restored to several East Riding villages by the building of bypasses. One of these is at Kirkburn, three miles southwest of Driffield, for this ancient community stands close to the busy A614 route from Goole to Bridlington and its picturesque church of St Mary's and its old cottages have been protected from the increasing traffic of modern times.

At the time of the *Domesday Book* the village was called Westburn, a name derived from the stream that is major feature of the village but became Kirkburn after the building of the church or kirk around 1130-1155. In fact the origins of the place are much older for in 1987 excavations there by British Museum archaeologists

St Mary's at Kirkburn is a fine Norman church built *c.* 1130. It is on the Sykes Churches Trail.

unearthed the grave of a warrior of the third century BC complete with a sword that has been described as 'probably the finest Iron Age sword in Europe'. The handle of this awesome weapon shows the great skill of the craftsmen of the time for it was constructed of thirty-seven pieces of iron, bronze, horn and red glass. The archaeological investigation revealed other details for the man (aged around thirty at the time of his death) had had three spears thrust into his chest as part of the funeral ritual. The nearby grave of a warrior of similar age was a 'chariot burial' of the same type as others in the East Riding with his chain-mail tunic draped over the corpse.

For anyone exploring Kirkburn today a visit to its famous Church of St Mary is a 'must' for this has been described as one of the two best examples of Norman churches in the East Riding. The church has a magnificent Norman doorway and there are unique figurative carvings on the font and an unusual tower staircase to see. By the eighteenth century the church was in a serious state of disrepair but underwent a major restoration in 1856-1857 thanks to the generosity of Sir Tatton Sykes of Sledmere. It was he who employed two of the leading church architects of the day, John Loughborough Pearson and George Edmund Street, to carry out the work.

In 1823 the population of Kirkburn was only 119 people and was still less than 200 by the end of the nineteenth century. Like most East Riding villages most of the people would have been engaged in farming or the rural occupations typical of self-reliant communities of the period. At the time of the 1851 census one of the farmers named was John Wheatley who employed nine labourers to carry out the labour intensive work involved on his farm of 408 acres while a directory of 1857 showed the presence in the village of Joseph Bowman (blacksmith), John Cobb (shoemaker) and Thomas and John Sheperdson (wheelwrights).

The same directory also named James Reed as a village carrier and shopkeeper and the 1861 census provides further details. This important historical record shows that James Reed, aged forty-two, was a grocer and wool-stapler. He had been born in Swanland around 1819 but his wife and five children had all been born in Kirkburn.

For villages not on the rail network carriers like James Reed performed a vital function in transporting goods by horse and cart to and from major centres of population and the 1857 directory shows that he provided a service to Beverley on Saturdays and Driffield on Thursdays. From a legal notice in the *London Gazette* we know that James Reed died on 20 February 1867 and that his widow, Bithia, and her children then continued the business. At the time of the 1871 census one of these children was James, a scholar aged ten, and the record shows that he went on to develop the family enterprise by moving to Driffield. An obituary in a local newspaper from 13 November 1943 marked the death of James Reed, 'one of Driffield's oldest tradesmen, aged eighty-three, founder of the firm of Reed's Stores, Market Place Driffield'. James Reed made his grocery business into a limited company and was active in the local community as 'a great supporter of the Driffield George Street Methodist Church and treasurer of the Driffield branch of the National Farmers Union'.

Above left: An artist's impression of the Kirkburn Sword by David Illingworth. *Image courtesy of David Illingworth*

Above right: One of the features of St Mary's Church at Kirkburn is this lovely Norman doorway. *Image courtesy of Jean Illingworth*

This cross was erected in 1910 by the second Sir Tatton Sykes to mark the spot of Kirkburn's famous elm tree (said to have been planted in 1688.) The tree grew to a circumference of 27 feet but blew down during a storm in 1907. According to local folklore treasure was supposed to have been buried underneath its roots!

Kirkburn's main street *c.* 1903. *Image courtesy of David Illingworth*

The Queen's Head public house *c.* 1902. *Image courtesy of David Illingworth*

Kirkburn Main Street looking towards the church *c.* 1900. *Image courtesy of David Illingworth*

The Sandhill plant of GWE Biogas Ltd produces methane-rich biogas from food waste and this is used to generate electricity. Government minister Lord Henley officially opened the plant in April 2011. *Image courtesy of Tom Megginson*

James Reed represented an upwardly mobile Kirkburn resident who through intelligence, ambition and hard work became rich and successful but there were many others who fared less well. The early 1840s were a time of particular economic hardship and became known as the 'hungry forties' with rising unemployment and high food prices. To feed their families some turned to crime and a local newspaper reported on 'nightly plunder' in this area of East Yorkshire during March 1842. On 11 March 1842 the *Hull Packet* said:

> Depredations continue almost nightly in the neighbourhood. On Thursday last the high barn of Mr Piercy of Kirkburn was visited by thieves and two pigs were slaughtered and taken away. Some tramps were sleeping in the barn and they say the thieves threatened to murder them if they gave alarm. There appears to be a regularly organised gang of thieves who seem to have free rein to rob the countryside with no police to apprehend them.

As a last resort villagers could look to the parish for support and Kirkburn, after 1836, became one of the forty-three parishes of the Driffield Poor Law Union. The cost of caring for paupers who because of factors like sickness, unemployment or old age could not support themselves was divided between the constituent parishes. The minute books of the Driffield Poor Law Guardians show that in September 1842 the ratepayers of Kirkburn made a quarterly payment £6 12s 0d as their share. A new Union Workhouse for 215 inmates was built in Driffield between 1866-1868 and one of its early residents was Frances Wood of Kirkburn aged seventy-five; she died there on 11 January 1869.

For the labouring class of Kirkburn, as elsewhere, the shame of becoming an inmate of the workhouse was ever present in the nineteenth century. Furthermore in the days before the Welfare State the services of a doctor were often beyond the financial reach of many families. A newspaper report of August 1888 for example reported on an enquiry into the death of the newly born child of William Cass of Kirkburn. The inquest recorded a verdict of 'death from want of proper attention at birth'. The 1891 census reveals that William Cass was an agricultural labourer (age forty) and that living with him in his cottage was his wife, his two children and his seventy-four-year-old mother-in-law who was 'paralysed'.

William Cass lived at Beckwatcher's Cottage and this was one of the estate houses built in the later nineteenth century by Sir Tatton Sykes, the Lord of the Manor. Even older was Kirkburn's public house called the 'Hare and Hounds' in a directory of 1823 and subsequently renamed the 'Queen's Head'.

Probably the greatest change seen in the village in recent times is Kirksburn's new £10 million renewable-energy power station opened in 2011. This was the inspiration of local farmers Tom Megginson and Mathew Girking and uses cutting edge technology to turn up to 50,000 tonnes of food waste a year into methane to generate electricity.

CHAPTER 19

North Dalton

For those who enjoy the quieter byways of East Yorkshire the beautiful landscape of the Yorkshire Wolds has long been a favourite of Sunday-afternoon motorists seeking an escape from the town or city. My own journey took me north from Beverley via Middleton-on-the-Wolds to the B1246 road which winds its way though North Dalton past its public house (the Star), its large pond (the Mere), its ancient church and along its main street. The name of this village, six miles southwest of Driffield, is thought to be derived from 'farmstead in a valley' and dates from Anglo-Saxon times even though there was human activity here much earlier. Among the archaeological discoveries made at North Dalton were a

The Star Inn at North Dalton was mentioned in a trade directory of 1823.

greenstone axe head and flint chisel from the Stone Age and funeral barrows from the Bronze Age.

The first documentary reference to North Dalton was in the *Domesday Book* when it was recorded that there were twenty-five villagers, three smallholders, a priest and a church. The Church of All Saints remains the oldest surviving building and stands on a mound at the centre of the village; parts of it (like the south doorway) date from the Norman period. North Dalton appears to have been a prosperous place during the Middle Ages and like other East Riding villages most of its people would have been engaged in farming under a communal system of open fields and common pastures. To make agriculture more efficient these were enclosed by Act of Parliament in 1779 and the village entered on a period of growth with many new houses and cottages being built.

By the time Edward Baines wrote about North Dalton in 1823 the population had risen to around 400 people and there were the usual trades of self-reliant communities of the time. These included two blacksmiths, two carpenters, two shoemakers, and three corn millers. From records in the East Riding Archive we know that North Dalton's Overseers of the Poor made provision for those who because of factors like ill-health, old age or unemployment could not support themselves. The village had its own poor house and a notice from April 1835 tells of the rules and regulations governing its operation. One of these was that 'the Governor or his wife shall, when any poor persons come into the house, carefully search them so that such persons and their clothes may be washed, cleansed and cured of filth and nastiness'.

Another, unpaid, parish official was the village constable charged with investigating crimes and arresting wrongdoers. From a coroner's inquest in September 1846 we know that William Smith was the name of North Dalton's constable in that year. A local newspaper says that it was Smith who investigated a suspicious death at North Dalton on 12 September 1846 and arrested a seventy-one year-old villager called Simon Griffin as the man responsible. There had been a quarrel between Griffin and a neighbour, thirty-five year old Elisha Brodrick, because of a dispute between their wives. An angry confrontation had taken place on the doorstep of Griffin's home with Brodrick threatening to put Mrs Griffin in the village pond. This had quickly turned to violence and in the ensuing struggle in the street outside Brodrick was stabbed by Griffin. The latter claimed that he was acting in self-defence for the much younger Brodrick 'had him by the throat and was throttling him' and that the deceased had fallen upon the knife and 'had caused his own death'. When the coroner's jury returned a verdict of manslaughter Griffin was remanded to stand trial at York Assizes. With the typical speed of nineteenth century justice the case was heard on 5 December 1846. Being a poor man Griffin could not afford legal representation and was undefended in court. Having listened to the evidence the jury found him guilty of manslaughter but recommended mercy on the grounds of provocation. The sentence was deferred

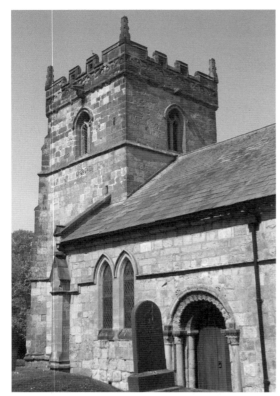

Left: The Church of All Saints dates back to Norman times and stands on a mound in the centre of the village.

Below: Westwood House was built around 1795 and was requisitioned by the government during the Second World War. During June and July 1944 it was used by officers of the Free French Second Armoured Division.

until 14 December when Judge Cresswell heeded the jury's advice and sentenced Griffin to six months' imprisonment.

By the time of the 1891 census the population of North Dalton had risen to 520 people with agriculture still the main occupation. Fourteen farmers were named in a directory of 1892 and they employed many others some of who lived in the 'hind houses' attached to farms. These labourers were often engaged on yearly contracts at the Driffield Hiring Fair during Martinmas week (November). Probably the hardest working women in North Dalton were the 'hind wives' (usually the farmers' wives) who were responsible for the boarding of the single men. Traditionally their busiest day was Monday 'wash day' when without the benefit of modern electrical appliances clothes had to be washed by hand using wash tubs, dolly sticks, mangles and muscle power.

During my visit to North Dalton I spoke to Ray Williams who has lived here for thirty years at Stephenson's Cottage, a lovely old property with beamed ceilings. Ray had a recording studio at home and around six years ago became involved in a project to preserve the memories of some of the village's oldest inhabitants. From these recordings a professional CD was made called *Looking Back* and this contains reminiscences of a time when the village had no running water and no electricity but still had three shops, two pubs, blacksmiths, tailors, cobblers and two chapels. Ray told me:

> I could not have done it without the help of North Dalton's oldest resident, Ted Duffill, a keen historian of the village, who encouraged his contemporaries to talk about their experiences.

Some of the reminiscences relate to the Second World War when the village became home to evacuee children from Hull and Sunderland and a training area for units of the British Army. The village hall was commandeered for use as a NAAFI to provide meals for these soldiers. After the 'Fall of France' in 1940, when there was a serious danger of a German invasion of eastern England, North Dalton had its own Home Guard unit. Ted Duffill was a member of this and recalled:

> There were about twenty of us and we were all issued with uniforms, rifles and ammunition. We were trained by regular soldiers in skills like map reading and were expected to go out on patrol. On one early morning patrol in May 1941 from a high vantage point near the village the fires raging in Hull after a heavy German bombing raid were clearly visible.

Other contributors to *Looking Back* recalled how the village was full of troops billeted at Tithe Farm and elsewhere, of tanks rumbling down the Main Street causing the stained-glass window at the east end of the church to fall out and of how the village pond area become a shooting range. In training for the Normandy

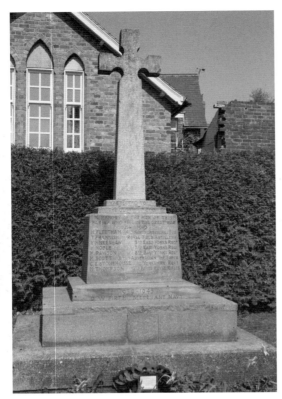

Left: The war memorial at North Dalton.

Below: This attractive barn conversion was once part of Tithe Farm.

The main street at North Dalton on a Spring day.

A view of the main street *c*. 1900 with the Methodist Chapel on the left.

A view of North Dalton's main street *c.* 1950 looking towards the school.

landings of 6 June 1944 tank drivers could be seen driving through hedgerows and fields of standing corn.

Another property requisitioned by the war department was Westwood House and its stable block became an ammunition store. From around 1 June to 20 July 1944 the house became a base for officers of the 'Free French' Second Armoured Division in training for the liberation of their homeland. Villagers recall seeing their fez-wearing Moroccan guards standing sentry at the entrances.

During my visit I spoke to Pat Gresham who has lived at Westwood House for over forty years. She told me that one of the French soldiers living there in 1944 was accused of being a 'spy', that he was court marshalled in an upstairs room with a villager as a witness to the proceedings and that he subsequently fell to his death from the landing. Pat firmly believes that it was the spirit of this dead soldier that haunted Westwood House in the early 1970s for she told me:

> The ghost seemed very attached to my small son Max who was playing with his toys in his room one day when he heard someone say his name. When he turned round he saw a big dark man who then disappeared through a wall! Babysitters reported that although they turned Max's bedroom light off it was then switched on again while he remained fast asleep. They said there was something spooky about the landing.

In the years since the Second World War North Dalton may have lost its shops but it does retain a thriving sense of community. Although farming no longer employs the numbers it once did other enterprises have developed. John Scott Engineering grew out of a village blacksmith's business while other enterprises include a music agency and a furniture restoration business. By the time of the 2001 census North Dalton Parish had a population of three hundred and fifteen and although there has been some new house building the character of this old village has been retained through the creation of a conservation area in 1977.

CHAPTER 20

Shiptonthorpe

Appearances can be deceptive and those travelling through Shiptonthorpe, two miles northwest of Market Weighton on the busy A1079 Beverley to York road, might be forgiven for thinking that this is a village blighted by the heavy traffic of modern times. Yet those who linger awhile to explore this ancient community on foot will discover on its side roads like Town Street and Station Road a more rural world comprising a complimentary mix of modern houses and several listed buildings, built in brick with pan-tile roofs, dating back to the eighteenth century. It is not surprising that the historic core of the village was designated as a conservation area in June 2010.

The busy A1079 road through Shiptonthorpe.

The name 'Shipton' comes to us from the Anglo-Saxon invaders of eastern England from the fifth century for the word is derived from *scaep* (meaning sheep) and *ton* meaning an enclosure. The nearby hamlet of Thorpe-le-Street explains the latter part of the place name although historical records usually referred to the village as Shipton until the twentieth century. However the origins of the village are in fact much older for archaeological investigations show that there was a community here in Roman times. Around the early second century AD the Romans had built a road from their fortress at Petuaria (Brough) to Eboracum (York) and the place where this road crossed Fox Beck was ideally suited for a settlement. Discoveries such as crop markings, coins, pottery and leather indicate the presence of a substantial roadside settlement while archaeologists discovered evidence of a large fourth-century Roman-style aisled hall some twenty-one metres long standing gable-end-on to the road itself. Interpretations of these and other discoveries (like quern stones used to grind cereals into flour) suggest that around twenty family groups of around four hundred and eighty people may have lived here by the end of the Roman occupation.

With an important road passing through it is not surprising that the village continued to be occupied after the departure of the Romans and further archaeological discoveries included a Saxon copper-alloy buckle and a sixth century cruciform brooch. Mentioned in the *Domesday Book* Shipton continued to benefit from its position on the main road to York and from the improvements brought about by a turnpike trust after 1764. When Edward Baines wrote about the village in 1823 Shipton had a population of three hundred and sixty nine people including eleven farmers, two butchers, a weaver, three shoemakers and a blacksmith.

The coming of the railway also benefited the inhabitants for the York to Market Weighton line was opened in October 1847 and Shipton had a conveniently-located station for both passengers and goods traffic. The line was the inspiration of York businessman George Hudson (nicknamed the Railway King) who in 1846 purchased the nearby Londesborough Estate. Hudson had his own private railway halt there but financial malpractice soon led to his ruin and he sold the estate in 1849. Shipton Station (later renamed Londesborough) benefited the local farming community with produce, especially vegetables, being moved to major centres of population especially when the line was extended from Market Weighton to Beverley in 1865. Until the growth of road freight after the First World War the railways continued to be the preferred way of moving goods and in 1913 alone twenty-eight wagons of livestock were loaded at the station. However this prosperity was not to last and competition from road transport led to a decline in receipts with the axing of goods traffic in May 1964 and the end of passenger services in November 1965. These days the former 'station house' (now a private residence) and a modern housing development called The Crossings remind us of the former importance of the place.

The Church of All Saints dates from the thirteenth century and was renovated in the sixteenth and nineteenth centuries. The medieval tower holds two bells. It is a Grade I listed building.

The former village school at Shiptonthorpe is now the village hall. A plaque on the side of the building records that the school was provided in 1893 'for the training of children in the principles of the Church of England'.

In the mid nineteenth century Shipton was a typical East Riding rural community dominated by the needs of farming. Among the census entries for the village in 1851 was that of John Brigham, age fifty-nine, a farmer of 100 acres. Living in more humble circumstances elsewhere was William Robinson, a thirty-six-year-old agricultural labourer. Interestingly the census shows that Robinson had a lodger called John Rolsey described as a 'farmer of eight acres at Shipton'. A blacksmith was an essential service in villages of the time for shoeing horses and repairing farm machinery and living on High Street was Richard Drake, a thirty-three-year-old blacksmith occupying five acres of land and employing one man. The 1851 census shows that Shipton had a number of paupers dependent on parish relief and one of these was Bertha Johnson, age thirty-two, described as 'a pauper of weak mind', while also living on High Street was Sarah Wharton, age sixty, described as a 'pauper shoemaker'. Shipton was part of the Pocklington Poor Law Union and some village paupers ended up in the Pocklington workhouse. The workhouse 'admission and discharge book' shows the presence there from 26 March to 11 June 1853 of Eliza Pearson from Shipton. She had sought admission because she was destitute and if this humiliation was not enough suffered the indignity of having the 'Number 4' affixed to her clothes.

By the year 1891 the population of Shipton had risen to 423 people and in common with many other East Riding villages its children could now benefit from an elementary education. A new village school supported by the Church of England was built in 1893 with accommodation for seventy children although by 1921 eighty-four children were on roll taught by the headteacher and two assistants. When Mr J. Moffat of the East Riding County Council visited Shipton School he pointed out the deficiencies of both the school buildings and the site they occupied saying:

> The site being somewhat of a shallow basin must be rather damp and dirty in winter. Perhaps this accounts for the many signs of dampness about the building. The main room is long and narrow without partition and occupied by two teachers. The out-offices are offensive.

Moffat was also increasingly critical of Shipton's head teacher Mr Smith describing him as 'very quiet, slow and sleepy' and with a teaching style with older pupils that was said to be 'dull and lifeless'. By July 1929 the outspoken inspector was prepared to go further when he wrote:

> The obvious weakness in this school is the fact the Headmaster has no real interest in his work. He follows a deadly dull routine and nags his pupils in a high-pitched voice. There is little attempt to stimulate real interest among the scholars.

This lovely whitewashed cottage can be found on Town Road and dates from the late eighteenth century.

Shiptonthorpe Methodist Chapel was built in the 1960s.

Langlands Garden Centre at Shiptonthorpe.

The Ve Raj Indian Restaurant on the A1709 road at Shiptonthorpe.

Shiptonthorpe (or Londesborough) Station was in use from 1847 to 1965. The stationhouse survives as a private residence and parts of the platforms are still visible in the back garden. *Image courtesy of the John Mann Collection*

In his reports Moffat also suggested that Shipton suffered from a lack of resources and clashes of personality among its school managers. On 15 January 1932 the inspector wrote:

> Today I called at the request of the vicar. He merely wished to go over old ground to tell me about all his troubles with regard to the rest of the school managers and how they packed their meetings and out-voted him.

It was perhaps with some relief to the inspector that Shipton's aging headmaster retired in 1934 and was replaced by a younger man, Mr Foster. However Moffat's initial praise soon turned to a more sober assessment for he wrote in 1938:

> Much of what he is doing seems to be ineffective. Firmer control and a more lively attack are necessary in his teaching. He is sleepy and dreamy in manner and there is little evidence of a bracing supervision of his assistants.

Shiptonthorpe Primary School closed in 1984 and these days village children are transported to a variety of other schools including those in Warter, Market

Weighton and Holme on Spalding Moor. However the old school has been put to good use as a village hall and £55,000 was spent refurbishing it in 2009.

Shiptonthorpe is now home to several successful businesses and chief among these is Langlands Gardens Centre. This grew from humble origins after the Second World War when Walter Ducker, began working at 'Langlands', the home of a West Riding mill owner, as a gardener, handyman and chauffeur. With a talent for growing dahlias, Walter Ducker bought his employer's nursery in 1955 and nine years later the business moved to a smallholding by the side of the A1069 at Shiptonthorpe and began to expand. These days this prosperous enterprise has a second garden centre near Leeds and its nurseries grow over a quarter of a million plants a year.

In the last fifty years Shiptonthorpe has seen many changes including, in recent times, the closure of its two public houses (the Crown and the Ship). Yet helped by an influx of younger people in the last ten years the village retains a tremendous sense of identity and community as shown by the multitude of sporting, cultural and social activities that take place here throughout the year.

CHAPTER 21

Burton Fleming

The study of place names can be a fascinating business and can reveal much about the origins of towns and villages. An interesting example of one such place name in East Yorkshire is 'Burton' and there are eight such examples in the county ranging from Bishop Burton near Beverley to Burton Pidsea in Holderness. The name *Burh-tun* come to us from the Angles, a Germanic tribe who settled in eastern England from the fifth century, and means a fortified village or farmstead. Burton Fleming, situated six miles northwest of Bridlington, was formerly known as North Burton and is one of the most northerly places in East Yorkshire. Burton Fleming was known by that name from at least the fourteenth century but its origins are even

St Cuthbert's Church dates back to the eleventh century. When weddings take place here there is an old custom of tying the churchyard gates together. The best man is expected to throw coins to waiting children in order that the gates can be opened.

older. There are pre-historic earthworks along part of the parish boundary with Hunmanby and archaeologists have uncovered iron-age burials too.

The centre of the village stands at the point where the Gypsey Race having flowed eastwards from its source turns south towards Rudston. In fact this is a rather intermittent watercourse and after periods of drought the streambed can be completely dry. Yet at other times, with the stream in full spate, the streets of Burton Fleming have been flooded. The most recent of these occasions came in December 2012 and January 2013 when after a period of heavy rain the Gypsey Race burst its banks and fifteen properties at centre of the village became flooded. According to Burton Fleming folklore such floods were often a portent of national disasters with the year of the Great Plague (1665) and the start of the Second World War (1939) being well-known examples.

Burton Fleming was mentioned in the *Domesday Book* when we are told that, prior to the Norman Conquest, 'Karli' had been the lord of the manor but that the land was now owned by King William. In the centuries that followed most people would have been engaged in farming or other related rural occupations under a system of open arable fields and common pastures until these were enclosed by act of parliament in 1769. At the time of the 1801 census the population was 237 people while a directory of 1823 provides us with the names of twelve farmers as well as other 'tradesmen' vital in such an isolated community as this.

The prosperity of this typical East Riding rural community is perhaps indicated by the fact that at the time of the 1851 census the population of the village had doubled. Census records provide a valuable 'snapshot-in-time' of villages in the late nineteenth century and that for Burton Fleming in 1881 provides us with details of those living there. Among these was William Richardson (age fifty-one) who lived at The Grange. He was described as a farmer of 350 acres employing five labourers and three boys. Meanwhile at Mill House Francis Thompson (age fifty-nine), a master miller from Beverley, performed the vital function of turning wheat into flour assisted by his twenty-five-year-old son William.

Back Street in Burton Fleming seems to have been the centre of working class life in the village and among those living there in 1881 was James Piercey (agricultural labourer) William Maynard (tailor), Jonathan Goforth (shoemaker) and George Thompson (saddler). A directory of 1892 also shows that the village population supported four grocer's and five 'carriers' linking the village with places on the rail network like Bridlington, Driffield, Filey and Scarborough.

It is an indication of the growth of Burton Fleming that more attention was paid to the education of its children. From the *Victoria County History* of the village we learn that in 1835 there were two day schools in the village educating twenty-three boys and twenty girls at their parents' expense although by 1868 it was said that 'all the farmers had governesses to teach their children at home'. National concerns about improving elementary education for the working classes led to the passing of an education act in 1870 and Burton Fleming established its own

One of Burton Fleming's two village ponds on Back Street. In the background is the old village schoolhouse (now closed).

The wide main street at Burton Fleming showing both old and new properties.

'school board' in 1873. This built a new school in Back Lane the following year. The school logbooks survive in the East Riding Archive in Beverley and provide a fascinating glimpse of life in a rural school in the early twentieth century. An entry from August 1903, for example, showed the kind of attendance problems typical of a time when children were often kept at home to undertake farm work or domestic chores. The schoolmaster wrote:

> Florrie Seeman has made fifteen attendances since May out of a possible ninety. Her brother Arthur has not made one.

On 12 May 1911 the schoolmaster wrote in the logbook:

> Eight boys were absent this afternoon killing mice for a farmer: Mr Sykes. They were not employed by him and were there against his wishes. The attendance officer caught the boys.

Distractions like Bridlington and Hunmanby Shows held in August affected attendance while outbreaks of infection had an effect too, for on 20 October 1911 the headteacher wrote:

> A poor attendance this week. There are four children ill with scarlet fever.

During the years after the First World War Burton Fleming School was visited regularly by the East Riding Schools' Inspector, Mr J. Moffat. In 1923 he reported that the school now had a new headmaster, Mr Thomas. The inspector reported in July 1923 that the headmaster was teaching the older pupils, Miss Hutchinson the younger ones while Miss Coates taught the infants class. However Moffat commented on the strained relationship between the headmaster and Miss Hutchinson for he wrote:

> For some time Mr Thomas has been dissatisfied with Miss Hutchinson's efforts. I don't think she is quite as bad as the headmaster makes out. I gather that owing to a quarrel in the village previous to Mr Thomas's arrival some of the Wesleyans have prejudiced the headmaster against her. He is said to treat Miss Coates as a favourite and Miss Hutchinson as the opposite.

Although Moffat said of the headmaster in July 1923 that Mr Thomas was 'settling down to his new appointment very satisfactorily', his initial praise turned to a more sober assessment for in April 1929 he wrote:

> The headmaster is most conscientious but he cannot be described as a very effective worker. Unfortunately he feels he is doing splendidly. Many of his aims are excellent but the pity is that he fails them by a big margin.

Left: The old village pump, Black Jack, with its two handles.

Below: Burton Fleming village hall.

The Burton Arms public house stands at the village crossroads.

Burton Fleming village store.

A tour of Burton Fleming today with its wide main street, its lovely church and its two village ponds makes it appear that this is a very tranquil place where nothing of significance ever happens. Yet appearances can be deceptive for in February 1995 the village was the scene of a brutal murder that made national headlines. A sixty-six-year-old local woman, Margaret Wilson, walking along a country lane near her home, had her throat cut in an apparently random and motiveless attack. Two farm workers witnessed the event, saw a man running down the lane after her and said that after murdering her he drove off in his car. Two years later a Driffield resident, Derek Christian, was found guilty of the crime and jailed for life. Since 1997 however doubts have been raised about the 'circumstantial' nature of the evidence against him culminating in a BBC programme on the case in 2004. In December 2007 it was announced that the case against Christian would be re-examined by the Criminal Review Cases Commission.

Unlike many other East Riding villages that have lost their local services Burton Fleming retains its public house, a village store/post office, a butcher's shop and a farmshop/tearoom. Increasing mechanisation on farms in Burton Fleming since the Second World War has meant that employment opportunities are now less than they were 100 years ago. In 1901 the population of the parish was 422 people but by the time of the 2001 census this had fallen to 363. However with new houses being built in the village in recent times Burton Fleming continues to attract newcomers and remains a very desirable place to live.

CHAPTER 22

Sewerby

At about 100 feet above sea level and with commanding views over Bridlington Bay the lovely village of Sewerby is a place whose virtues only became known to a much wider audience from the nineteenth century with the arrival of the railway. The Hull to Scarborough line opened in October 1846 and with stations at Bridlington and nearby Marton day-trippers from the West Riding and further away began to appreciate the beauty of the Yorkshire coast. Before then Sewerby would have remained a small, fairly isolated village dominated by the needs of farming and other rural occupations.

The name Sewerby is probably of Danish origin and thought to be derived from 'Syward's farmstead'. This part of the Yorkshire coast was subject to invasion

The main street of Sewerby.

from the fifth century AD after the departure of the Romans and archaeological investigations at Home Farm, Sewerby have revealed numerous artefacts from an Anglian cemetery there dating from the sixth century AD. These include objects like brooches, buckles, bracelets and pottery bowls. The village was mentioned in the *Domesday Book* when it was recorded that Sewerby had been owned by individuals called Carle and Torchil but the land was now 'waste' following the 'Harrying of the North' by William the Conqueror between 1069 and 1071.

Estate papers held by the Hull History Centre show that the manor of Sewerby was in the hands of the de Sewerdby family from at least the twelfth century until the sixteenth century. They would have lived in a manor house on the site of the present Sewerby Hall. This was the eighteenth century creation of John Graeme (1664-1746) from a wealthy family of Bridlington merchants who bought the Sewerby estate around 1714. In the years that followed he created a house of great elegance and among its original Georgian features is a cantilever staircase hand-built in oak. Sewerby Hall continued in the possession of the Graeme family and there was further work in the Regency and Victorian periods including an Orangery in the mid nineteenth century, a clock tower in 1847 and a gatehouse in 1848.

As Lords of the Manor the Graeme family would have exerted a powerful influence on the village of Sewerby itself. The villagers of Sewerby were fortunate in that they continued to benefit from the generosity of later occupants of the 'big house'. Local newspapers from 1854 and later record that there was a distribution of blankets, warm clothing, beef, coals and other items around Christmas to cottagers in the village.

At the time of the 1801 census the population of Sewerby was that there were seven farmers/yeomen together with the usual trades of self reliant communities of the time like a blacksmith, a shoemaker, a wheelwright and a corn miller. Village trades were often passed on from father to son and in 1823 Francis Hodgson was the blacksmith while the 1871 census shows that his thirty-year-old son was continuing the tradition.

Tragically newspapers of the time often recorded the attempts of unmarried women to conceal unwanted pregnancies for fear of being dismissed from their jobs. The *Hull Packet* newspaper of 4 August 1865 reported on an inquest held at the house of Robert Wise, a Sewerby farmer, on the body of a newborn female child that had been found in a box in a bedroom. The jury gave the verdict that the child had been smothered at birth but at Bridlington Magistrates Court the local surgeon who had carried out the post-mortem was now less sure. He was there to give evidence in the case of Tamar Redhead from Flamborough, a thirty-one year employee of Robert Wise, who was charged with 'concealing the birth of her female child on the 25th of July'. Since murder was a hanging offence the surgeon merely said that if the child had breathed, 'before or after the birth he could not say', and that there were no signs of external violence on the child. Nevertheless

The Ship Inn on Back Lane Sewerby. In 1823 the village pub was called the Bottle and Glass but was rebuilt in 1846 as the Ship Inn. It was sold to the Hull Brewery Company in 1937. These days the pub hosts a ten-day beer and music festival in August–September.

As the name suggests the Old Forge tearoom was once the blacksmith's shop at Sewerby. Note the use of chalk and cobbles in its construction.

Above left: Sewerby Hall. This was built between 1714 and 1720 for John Greame.

Above right: After her famous flight to Australia (5–24 May 1930) Amy Johnson became a national hero. She performed the opening ceremony at Sewerby Hall on 1 June 1936 and the 'Amy Johnson Room' was later created there in her honour.

Sewerby Hall during the heavy snow of November–December 2010 through the lens of Merice Marshall. *Image courtesy of Merice Ewart Marshall*

Right: 'Splash of Gold-Sewerby Cliffs' is a painting by Glenn Marshall, *Image courtesy of Glenn Marshall*

Below: A postcard of Sewerby village in 1943. *Image courtesy of Craig Bradley /Colin Breeze*

Sewerby Post Office *c.* 1910. Also shown are the premises of George Chadwick, bootmaker. *Image courtesy of Craig Bradley/ Colin Breeze*

concealing the birth of a baby was considered a serious offence and the woman was bailed to appear at York Assizes. When she was tried there in March 1866 Tamar Redhead pleaded guilty and was sentenced to two months' imprisonment.

A contemporary account of Sewerby in the 1920s held by the East Riding Museum Service shows how primitive life could be at that time. These childhood reminiscences tell us:

> There was no running water. The bottom half of the street had to fetch water from a pump at the top of Castle Garth and the top end of the street from a pump in the hall grounds by the head gardener's bungalow. Everyone had a well in their back garden and from this we used to take water for washing clothes on Monday. My first job on arriving at the house was to go to the joiner's shop for some paraffin for the lamps. There was no electric then.

With the arrival of cheaper motoring from the 1930s Sewerby began to attract greater numbers of visitors and residents drawn to the natural beauty of this seaside village. Estates of bungalows and chalets were built between the village and the sea. A newspaper clipping from 10 February 1934 under the headline 'Sewerby shows the way' described the first stage in an 'ambitious plan' to create the North Cliff Estate of nineteen bungalows for £375 each (plus £10 a year ground rent) that were to be 'perfect models of all that is best in modern architecture and enlightened hygiene'. The article went on to describe the allure of the location by saying:

Each bungalow is so situated that from its windows or verandah the occupants command a view of the large expanse of water which breaks against the ninety high feet cliffs on which the estate is being built.

The year 1934 was indeed a momentous one for the village for it also saw the sale of Sewerby Hall to Bridlington Corporation and the beginnings of its transformation into a major tourist attraction for the area. On 1 June 1936 a crowd of about 10,000 people watched the famous aviator Amy Johnson perform the opening ceremony. In the years after the Second World War her name and that of the hall became increasingly linked when the Amy Johnson Room was created to house the memorabilia donated by Amy's father in 1958. The creation of this room was only one of the ways that this fine building was put to good use for it also became a museum on the history and landscape of the East Riding and an art gallery. These days Sewerby Hall and Gardens is one of East Yorkshire's most popular tourist attractions bringing in over one hundred and fifty thousand visitors each year. In September 2011 multi-million pound proposals were unveiled by East Riding County Council to restore and enhance this valuable asset.

CHAPTER 23

Molescroft

It is one of the features of urban expansion that villages that were once unique entities have become absorbed by larger neighbours. This process can be seen at Beverley where for the wealthy it became fashionable to move away from the town centre and into the countryside with the development of New Walk and the rising ground of Molescroft. While ribbon development began along Molescroft Road from the late 1920s it was not until after the Second World War that this formerly tiny village (with only 111 people living there in 1823) saw a huge population growth. In the last sixty years Beverley's northern suburb of Molescroft has become a very desirable place to live and with its new housing estates has become

The Molescroft Inn. There was a licensed house at Molescroft from 1754. During the nineteenth century the public house here was known by several names including the Wellington, the Trafalgar and the Grapes.

one of the fastest growing localities in East Yorkshire. By the time of the 2001 census Molescroft Parish had a population of 6,810.

Molescroft probably had its origins as an Anglian settlement from the sixth century and the name may be derived from 'Mul's enclosure'. The original village, close to where the Molescroft Inn stands today, was located in a small valley cut into the Wolds and lay at the junction of roads to Beverley, Malton and Driffield. Mentioned in the Domesday Book of 1086 Molescroft would have been a small, typical farming community with its open arable fields located on the higher ground and the commons, pastures and carrs on the lower, more waterlogged land, to the east. The Molescroft Enclosure Act was passed in 1801 and in a directory of 1823 four farmers were named although none of the other usual trades (like blacksmith) typical of larger villages of that time. However since the village was strategically positioned at an important road junction it did support a public house and in the 1823 directory Francis Johnson was named as the licensee of the 'Wellington' (later the Molescroft Inn).

The routes north from Molescroft to Bainton (on the Malton Road) and to Driffield via Leconfield were controlled after 1766 by a turnpike trust and there was a tollhouse in south Molescroft (near Gallows Lane) to collect money from road users. Paying tolls was hugely unpopular and some tried to avoid them by using Pighill Lane (later Woodall Way) to enter Beverley thereby circumventing the Molescroft Bar. In 1769 therefore it was ordered this avoiding route should be 'stopped up' with rails and a gate. Another way of evading the tolls was for travellers to leave their horses and vehicles at the Molescroft public house and walk into Beverley and so a new tollhouse was erected at the Malton-Driffield junction in 1852 to prevent this.

By the time of the 1891 census the population of Molescroft had risen only slightly to one hundred and ninety six inhabitants with farming still predominant. Constitution Hill Farm on the Malton Road was one of those mentioned in a directory of 1892 and in February 1917 it was the scene of a brutal murder that made national headlines. The victim was thirteen-year-old Lily Tindale, the daughter of farm baliff John Tindale. She was described as 'a smart well developed girl who looked several years older than her age'.

On the afternoon of Thursday 15 February 1917 John Tindale discovered the body of his daughter in the stackyard of the farm under a pile of loose straw with 'her throat shockingly cut and her clothing covered with blood and dirt'. Suspicion about the murder soon fell on a shepherd called John Thompson who had gone missing immediately afterwards. A manhunt was quickly launched at nearby Beverley and he was arrested there the same evening. The most damning evidence against Thompson at the time of his arrest was his bloodstained hands and clothes. Upon examination Thompson's trousers were so soaked with blood that his knees were stained with it. There was also blood on his clay pipe, his pocket-knife and between the fingers of his hands.

Above: The Church of St Leonard at Molescroft was opened in 1896. To cater for Molescroft's growing population in the 1960s and 1970s the church was extended with the work completed in 1979.

Left: An account of the 'Molescroft Murder' (15 February 1917) in the *Weekly Dispatch* newspaper.

BRUTAL MURDER ON A YORKSHIRE FARM

Little Girl of Thirteen the Victim.

The brutal murder and mutilation of a 13-year-old girl were described in Beverley Police Court yesterday, when John William Thompson, 42, a shepherd, was charged with the crime and remanded for a week.

The victim was Lucy Tindale, the daughter of John Tindale, of Constitution Hill Farm, where the accused worked.

The father of the girl between his sobs related how he was called from his work in the fields because his daughter was missing. He searched the farm buildings and plantation and eventually found her body in a straw yard buried beneath some straw. Her throat was cut and near by was a part of a razor case said to belong to the prisoner, upon whom suspicion fell, as he had left his sheep and the farm.

The evidence of Police-Sergeant Jackson showed that the girl had made a terrible struggle for life. She was lying on straw saturated with blood. Her body had been mutilated.

Charged with murder and undefended, Thompson appeared in front of East Riding magistrates. Satisfied that there was a case to answer Thompson was remanded in custody and removed to Hedon Road Prison in Hull to await further court appearances. With the committal proceedings over Thompson was sent for trial to the York Assizes where he appeared in front of Judge McCardie on 9 March 1917. The case took less than one day. Thompson, being a poor shepherd, could not afford representation and so the judge asked a Mr Paley-Scott to defend him. The prosecution barrister quickly established the overwhelming evidence indicating Thompson's guilt. The only chance that Paley-Scott had in saving his client from the gallows was to convince the jury that Thompson was insane. He argued that Thompson's actions, in view of the extraordinary ferocity involved in slaying Lily Tindale in such a brutal fashion indicated he was suffering from 'homicidal mania'. However, his arguments failed to sway the jury who, after only nineteen minutes' deliberation, found Thompson guilty of wilful murder. Judge McCreadie too showed no hesitation when he sentenced him to death by hanging. Thompson, who had maintained an attitude of stolid indifference throughout, took the sentence calmly and was hurried away. He was then sent to Armley Prison in Leeds where he was executed on 27 March 1917.

By the beginning of the twentieth century Molescroft Road was already established as a desirable residential area and census records provide us with details of the professional classes living there. One of these at the time of the 1911 census was Alfred Beaumont, the County Surveyor for the East Riding, who lived at Elmcroft while Elmsall Lodge was the residence of Harry Wray, a Driffield-born solicitor, and his three daughters. One of the most significant properties was Longcroft Hall at the top of Gallows Lane owned by John Anthony Hudson an East Riding JP. With its extensive grounds overlooking the Westwood this was clearly a house to aspire to and in 1934 was purchased by the Beverley industrialist Gordon Armstrong for the sum of £3,250. Armstrong had made his fortune as a munitions' manufacturer during the First World War and by making shock absorbers at his Eastgate factory in the inter-war years. An order from the motor manufacturer William Morris in 1929 enabled him to expand his business and helped to make Beverley a more prosperous place during the depression years of the 1930s. Gordon Armstrong was also one of Beverley's great benefactors supporting fund-raising for the town's cottage hospital (1938) and during the Second World War he established a mobile canteen in the market place serving free cups of tea and coffee to anyone in uniform.

Gordon Armstrong left Beverley in 1944 and Longcroft Hall later became part of Beverley College (1960). In fact it is a good indication of the growth of Molescroft that a village that had no school at all in 1945 now has a college, two primary schools and Longcroft School and Performing Arts College (established in 1949). The need for improved education is shown by the increase in Molescroft's population: 2,738 people in 1971. By then large numbers of new houses had been

Above: Longcroft Hall on Gallows Lane later became a part of Beverley College.

Left: Gordon Armstrong (1885-1969) was a leading Beverley industrialist. On the 31 October 1934 he bought Longcroft Hall from John Harold Hudson for £3,250.

THIS CAR CAN BE YOURS!

The accompanying photograph is a model of the Morris Eight Saloon Car, Series I., in blue, with blue upholstery, which has been given by Mr Gordon Armstrong, the well-known Beverley and Hull motor dealer, to help the funds of the Beverley Carnival and Shopping Week in aid of the Hospital.

This car, which is an absolutely up-to-the-minute production from the Morris works, combines all the valuable features of recent models with the latest innovations in the way of security, roominess, comfort, speed and action.

It does not differ in general design from a big car. It possesses a sound and exceptionally efficient four-cylinder water-cooled engine, with a totally enclosed three-speed synchromesh gear-box.

Special features of the car are its generous dimensions, hydraulic shock absorbers, hydraulic brakes, and rear axle of three-quarter floating type.

The car, which will be supplied complete with buffers front and rear, and electric traffic indicators, is valued at £128, and every person who fills in a coupon, selecting from 30 suggestions, the ten vegetables most suitable for hospital patients, stands an equal chance of winning this car for the outlay of a modest sixpence.

This Morris Eight is extremely economical to run, and its calls would not be beyond the poorest. The total road tax for the year is only £6, and the petrol consumption is just 45 miles to the gallon.

The car is capable of travelling at a speed of 60 miles an hour, and will seat four adults as comfortably as any bigger vehicle.

Coupons, which are priced at sixpence each, may be obtained from any of Messrs Gordon Armstrong's business establishments in Beverley or Hull, or from any member of the Carnival Committee. They should be filled in and returned as indicated on the coupon, where fuller particulars are also printed, as early as possible.

In the days before the NHS, fundraising by the local community helped to support cottage hospitals. Here is an advertisement from a local newspaper of 1938 for a 'win-a-car' competition 'to help the funds of the Beverley Carnival in aid of the hospital'. The Beverley industrialist Gordon Armstrong donated the prize, a Morris 8 car.

Bungalows of the late 1960s built in Wheatlands Drive, Molescroft.

Woodhall Way (previously Pighill Lane) saw some house building in the 1930s and this gathered pace in the 1960s. Molescroft Parish Council dates from 1937.

Beverley's north east bypass (Grange Way) opened up a large area of Molescroft for new housing development after 1995. Shown on the right is the Hayride Public House opened in 1997.

built in the area between Molescroft Road and Woodall Way. A sales brochure from 1963 held by the East Riding Archive in Beverley shows that Stepney Contractors were building 'beautifully planned and expensively equipped bungalows and houses at prices ranging from £2,525 to £3,575 at Molescroft Park'.

To the east of Woodall Way another new estate was built off Copandale Road in the 1980s. The continued expansion of Molescroft remains a controversial subject among those living there for the completion of the north eastern bypass (Grange Way) in 1995 opened up a huge new area of land around Lockwood Road for housing. Meanwhile it is claimed that plans for a north western bypass at Molescroft will lead to the disappearance of sixteen acres of agricultural land in order to build 150 new homes.

CHAPTER 24

Harpham

For motorists exploring the picturesque beauty of the northern Yorkshire Wolds it is sometimes easy to miss some of the areas prettiest villages if these are situated off the major routes. Those who regularly travel on the A614 road to Bridlington may have seen signposts to Harpham, five miles northeast of Driffield, but how many will have been here to see this lovely village? Those who do are in for a real treat for there are a number of fascinating legends associated with the place as well as a lovely church to explore and a welcoming public house to visit. Harpham is the reputed birthplace of St John of Beverley. In the Middle Ages his tomb at Beverley Minster became an important centre of pilgrimage while St John's Well at Harpham was associated with miraculous powers of healing.

The St Quintin Arms Inn dates back to at least 1600.

Although the musical-sounding name 'Harpham' probably comes to us from the Norse invaders of eastern England and may mean the 'homestead of a harper', archaeological evidence suggests there was settlement here much earlier. The village lies on a spring-line of the Yorkshire Wolds and a ready supply of fresh water made it attractive to both Celtic people and Romano-Britons. In 1904 a local clergyman unearthed mosaic floors and other artefacts from a Roman villa of the third century AD.

In the turbulent centuries of invasion that followed the departure of the Romans we know little of events at Harpham other than legends associated with St John of Beverley who is said to have been born in the village to noble parents around AD 640. Visitors to Harpham will have seen 'St John's Well' which originated, according to legend, when this saintly churchman banged his staff on the ground to provide water for the army of a British prince trying to escape from pursuing Norsemen. In the years that followed the well became associated with the cult of St John and his miraculous powers of healing. According to local tradition the well water had fertility benefits and could provide a 'cure' for headaches and other ailments as well as having a soothing effect on wild animals! As the founder of Beverley Minster, an important place of pilgrimage during the Middle Ages, St John's reputation as a healer grew.

As befitting Harpham's links with the patron saint of the deaf and dumb throughout the world, the well is the scene each May of an important ceremony to mark 'St John of Beverley Day'. Joy Anslow a retired churchwarden who has lived in Harpham for twenty years told me about it:

> The choir of Beverley Minster, their parents, villagers and sightseers gather at the church and walk in procession to St John's Well. This has already been 'dressed' with flowers by local children and there is then a service at the church followed by a generous supper.

The Church of St John remains the oldest surviving structure at Harpham with Norman masonry still visible in the external walls of the nave and the chancel. The outstanding feature of the church is the north chapel with its tombs and monuments of the St Quintin family who as the major landowners dominated Harpham for centuries. The name is said to come from the town of St Quintin in France and a family tradition says that it was Herbert St Quintin who accompanied William the Conqueror to England in 1066 and fought alongside him at the Battle of Hastings. As a reward the St Quintins were given extensive lands in the East Riding and Harpham was to become the centre of their estates with a manor house being built there. All that remains today are earthworks and the vestiges of the fishponds near the church for in the seventeenth century Henry St Quintin moved the family to Scampston, near Malton. However the continuing importance of the St Quintins to the people of Harpham is shown by a newspaper report of

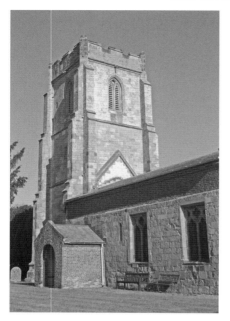

Above left: The Church of St John at Harpham was begun in Norman times. The north chapel contains monuments to the St Quintin family.

Above right: A stained glass window of St John at Beverley Minster.

The Well of St John at Harpham has a reputation for miraculous powers of healing and in May each year there is a well dressing ceremony here in celebration of Harpham's most famous son.

April 1872 on the festivities at Scampston Hall on the coming of age of William Herbert St Quintin. To mark his twenty-first birthday their tenants at Harpham and elsewhere were transported by special train from Lowthorpe Station and then to Scampston Hall for two days of extravagant celebrations including musical performances, a dinner, a ball and a fireworks display. Nor were the more humble of Harpham's residents, the cottage tenants, ignored for on the second day they were transported to Scrampston too and 'treated to dinner, tea and a variety of games and amusements'.

A visit to Harpham Church to see to influence of the St Quintin family on the village is therefore to be recommended. The earliest of the monuments is the alabaster tomb of William St Quintin who died in 1349 and the pedigree of the family, unbroken for seven centuries, is also represented in stained glass. Behind the church is another of Harpham's famous wells, the 'Drummer's Well' associated with a legendary story concerning the St Quintins. Local folklore recounts the tale of a fourteenth-century drummer boy called Tom Hewson who was accidentally knocked down the well by a member of the St Quintin family. According to the story Tom's mother was a witch who put a curse on the St Quintin family and predicted that when one of their number was about to die the sound of Tom's drum would be heard from the bottom of the well.

Throughout its history Harpham would have remained a typical agrarian village and in common with places elsewhere in the East Riding its people would have been engaged in farming under an open field system until these were enclosed by act of parliament in 1773. Eight farmers were named in a directory of 1823 and the village had the usual trades of self-reliant communities of the time like a blacksmith, a wheelwright, a tailor and two shoemakers. The Ellyard family were important farmers at Harpham and were wealthy enough to employ domestic servants. In 1870 one of these, Ann Holiday, age eighteen, was working for Nicholas Ellyard and was charged with 'concealing the birth of a child by throwing it into a stream at Harpham on the 15th of March'. She denied causing the death of her baby but was committed to stand trial at York in August. Considered to be a "young woman of weak intellect" she was sentenced to one month's imprisonment for her crime. Nicholas Ellyard himself met a tragic end in May 1884. The eighty-four-year-old farmer was gored by a bull when he tried to drive the animal away from a fence adjoining the village school where it was being teased by the children.

Harpham's farmers would have benefited from the coming of the railway when the Hull to Bridlington line opened in October 1846 for there was a station at Lowthorpe only a mile or so from Harpham. What the village did have however was a level crossing on the minor road from Harpham to Gransmoor and this was the scene of a tragic car accident on 15 November 1936 when the Scarborough to Hull train travelling at about 55 mph collided with an Alvis car driven by Harold Gee, a Hull merchant. Both he and his twelve-year-old son were killed

The junction of the main street and Station Road at Harpham.

The village hall for Harpham and Lowthorpe was built in 1933.

A beautiful eighteenth-century whitewashed farmhouse at Harpham.

Daggett Lane at Harpham. A date plaque on one of the cottages here shows that it was built in 1775.

in the accident and a subsequent report by the Ministry of Transport said that, 'as a result of the collision, the car was completely wrecked and its chassis was carried along by the engine for a distance of about half a mile, until the train came to a standstill'. The enquiry pointed to a number of factors in the tragedy. These included the fact that the locks on the crossing gates were broken and therefore the gates could be operated by impatient road users, a failure of the crossing-gate keeper to notice that a car was on the line until it was too late and a failure of the occupants of the car to look out for trains before crossing.

At the time of the 2001 census Harpham parish had a population of 318 people and agriculture remains an important part of its economy. One of the attractions of a visit to Harpham is its public house the St Quintin Arms, while the village hall is used for activities such as bingo, family parties and jumble sales.

CHAPTER 25

Bilton

It is one of the features of urban expansion that villages that were once unique entities have either been absorbed by larger neighbours or are now barely distinguishable from them. In the case of Hull places like Sculcoates and Drypool were gradually swallowed up by a relentless suburban growth that began in the late eighteenth century and are now firmly within the city. Bilton, five miles east of Hull City Centre, remains mostly part of the East Riding but other parts now lie within Hull. This popular suburban settlement saw tremendous growth both before and after the Second World War. In 1921 the population of Bilton Parish was only 127 people but by the time of the 2001 census this had grown to 2,340.

The B1238 road through Bilton. The civil parish of Bilton consists of Bilton, Ganstead and Wyton.

Extensions to the city boundary beginning in 1930 took away acreage from the village to feed Hull's insatiable appetite for more land. In 1936 Hull Corporation bought part of Bilton Grange Farm and soon after announced plans to create an estate of eight hundred houses there.

The origins of Bilton can be traced back to at least Anglo-Saxon times and the name is thought to come from 'Billa's Farm'. Mentioned in the Domesday Book the village remained a tiny place dominated by the needs of farming and the population in 1821 was only ninety-one people. What set Bilton apart however was its importance in the communications of the time for it lay on the circuitous main road from Hull to Hedon via Bilton and Preston before a more direct route along the bank of the Humber was created after 1830. Edward Baines, writing in 1823 said of Bilton:

> It is a small though pleasant village healthily situated and on account of its vicinity to Hull and being immediately in the public road land conveyances of every kind pass and re-pass daily.

Being on a major route however carried with it onerous responsibilities for under the Highways Act of 1555 the parishioners of Bilton, like those elsewhere, were made responsible for the maintenance of the roads. They had to elect a Surveyor of Highways annually and under his direction spend six days each year repairing the roads, with no financial gain. This system of 'statute labour' was particularly difficult at a place like Bilton where the low-lying nature of the land meant that the road had to be raised on a causeway to prevent it flooding. Under the act local Justices of the Peace were told to inspect the roads and the courts could punish parishes that neglected their duties. From records in the East Riding Archive in Beverley we know that in 1707 that the inhabitants of Bilton were indicted for the non-repair of a highway called 'Armitage Cawsey' and there were further indictments in 1717, 1738 and 1743.

Such was the importance of the route from Hull to Hedon via Bilton that it was one of the first in the East Riding to be taken over by a 'turnpike trust' (1745). They were given the responsibility of improving the road but made travellers pay a toll for using it. One of the tollhouses was at Wyton Holmes near Bilton where a coach pulled by six horses had to pay six old pence with varying charges for other road users. From old newspapers we learn that the right to collect the tolls here was auctioned off to the highest bidder. At the auction of 21 February 1862 the Wyton Holmes toll bar was let to the existing tenant, John Bower of Hunslet near Leeds, for £230. From census records we know that he delegated William Wright, from Bradford, as his 'collector of highway tolls'. Road tolls on this route were not abolished until 1878 when growing competition from the railways made turnpike trusts increasingly uneconomic.

Although Bilton remained a fairly small village in the nineteenth century it did support a church school. A new schoolroom and master's house was built in 1869

Hull's first Asda Superstore at Bilton. It was granted planning permission in March 1981 and opened later that year.

A milestone on the main road through Bilton. The village lay on the important route from Hull to Hedon via Preston.

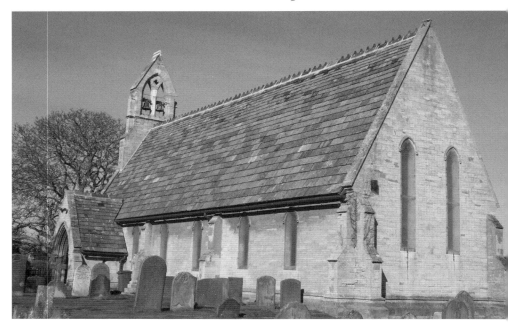

St Peter's Church at Bilton was designed by G. T. Andrews and built in 1851.

Bilton Village Hall was opened in 1986 and was paid for by £21,000 raised by the village together with grant aid from Holderness Borough Council and Humberside County Council. It replaced an earlier wooden structure erected in 1932.

Bilton Theatre is the home of the Bilton Amateur Dramatic Society.

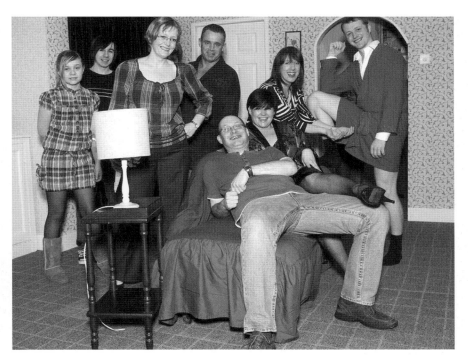

The cast and crew of *Anyone For Breakfast?* in February 2009. *Image courtesy of the Bilton Amateur Dramatic Society*

Older houses on the main road through Bilton.

Wyton Holmes Toll Bar House pictured *c.* 1908. The house was at the junction of Bilton, Sproatley and Preston roads. At the time of the 1861 census William Wright, age forty-three, lived here and was described as a 'collector of highway tolls'.

and the school logbook survives in the East Riding Archive in Beverley. This tells us that a new headmaster, Joseph Fell, arrived in November 1893 to take charge and like many of his kind he was soon complaining about the attendance problems that were commonplace when children were expected to undertake farm work. On 31 July 1895 he wrote:

> There has been poor attendance each day during the month. The school attendance committee have given permission to each child to work in the turnip fields and advantage has been taken of this to keep children at home who are not working in the fields.

Joseph Fell was still the headmaster at Bilton when the East Riding Schools' Inspector, Mr J. Moffat, visited the school in May 1921. The number of pupils at that time was only thirty-five with Mr Fell teaching the older pupils and Miss Broadbent the younger ones. The inspector wrote:

> It is refreshing to visit Mr Fell's school as he is so unlike the majority of headmasters. Being rather unorthodox in his methods and somewhat of a wag one is apt to overlook his deficiencies. He is very easy going and confesses he is lazy but I feel sure he is not so bad as he pretends to be.

While Joseph Fell was now aged sixty-two and had told the inspector that he was considering retirement he was still there in January 1925. Although he died shortly afterwards Bilton Church of England School continued to thrive and saw a rapid increase in the number of children attending from 1930 when new housing schemes in the village saw an influx of families. Between 1934 and 1937 the numbers attending rose from sixty eight to 121.

After the Second World War Bilton continued to prosper with new housing developments in the 1960s like the Lime Tree Lane Estate. It did however remain a close-knit village with a great sense of community involvement and must be unique among places in the East Riding in that it has its own theatre operated by the Bilton Amateur Dramatic Society. The origins of the society can be traced back to 1946 when a group of residents decided to put on a pantomime for their children. Such was their enthusiasm for amateur dramatics that by 1951 they had taken over an old recreation hall and began converting it into a proper theatre with a stage and dressing rooms. The first play performed there was *Elizabeth the First* in 1953.

CHAPTER 26

Burton Agnes

Each year over a thousand jazz enthusiasts flock to Burton Agnes Hall to enjoy three days of performances by some of Britain's most talented vocalists and musicians. Those who arrive for these events are able to admire one of the great country houses of Yorkshire and the treasures it contains and also to savour a village of great antiquity.

The name 'Burton' comes to us from Anglo-Saxon times and means a fortified village or farmstead while the suffix 'Agnes' is thought to be derived from a twelfth-century Lady of the Manor, Agnes of Aumale. Around the year 1170 a manor house was built there and this rare Norman survival, its vaulted under croft

Burton Agnes Hall was built 1601-1610 for Sir Henry Griffith to a design by Robert Smithson, the leading architect of his time. This image is from *A Series of Picturesque Views of Seats of Noblemen and Gentlemen of Great Britain and Ireland courtesy of the Noel collection at www.jamessmithnoelcollection.org*

and massive stone piers supporting the hall above, is these days a Grade I listed building under the guardianship of English Heritage. Behind the manor house is another rarity: a seventeenth century tread-wheel once worked by a donkey and used to pull water up from a well.

In the more peaceful times of the early seventeenth century wealthy landowners were able to build grander houses of greater style and comfort. In 1601 a new manor house was commissioned by Sir Henry Griffith and designed by Robert Smithson, the master mason of Queen Elizabeth I.

Burton Agnes Hall remains one of the great architectural gems of East Yorkshire and one of its glories is the south-facing long gallery which originally went across the whole length of the second floor and is renowned for its decorative plaster work. The hall stands on rising ground above the village with superb views to the coast and in 1697 was visited by the noted travel writer Celia Fiennes who said that from the gallery windows you could 'view the whole country round and discover the ships under sail though at a good distance'.

Another claim to fame of Burton Agnes Hall is a legendary ghost story about a screaming skull dating from 1620. Ann Griffith, the youngest of the three daughters of Sir Henry Griffith had been on a visit to nearby Harpham when she was attacked and robbed by ruffians. According to the macabre story she was brought back to Burton Agnes to die but pleaded that after her demise her head should be severed from her body and preserved within the hall. In the event her wishes were at first ignored and she was laid to rest in the churchyard. However when her vengeful spirit returned to torment her relatives the story says that her grave was re-opened and her skull returned to the house. Any attempt to move it elsewhere, it is claimed, meant a return of her noisy and restless spirit and so the skull was encased in a wall so that it could never be removed.

Sir Henry Griffith died in 1654 and Burton Agnes Hall passed to the Boynton Family and has remained in their hands ever since. Simon Cunliffe-Lister, the current owner, inherited the estate from his uncle Marcus Wickham-Boynton who died childless in 1989. Like the owners of other estates in the East Riding the Boynton Family have for centuries exerted a powerful influence on the village, its inhabitants and their employment. It was Sir Henry Boynton, for example, who built a new school for the village on Rudston Road in 1871. An analysis of the information provided by the 1901 census is particularly revealing. Living at Burton Agnes Hall with Thomas Boynton (age thirty-one), his wife and their six-month-old son were eight domestic servants including a housekeeper, a footman, two housemaids and a nurse. Living elsewhere in the village were other employees like the butler (Charles Heptonstall), a coachman, a gardener and three grooms.

Today the Burton Agnes Estate owns many of the surrounding farms and houses and at the hall itself there are fifty staff including guides, gardeners and cleaners to meet the needs of one East Yorkshire's most popular tourist attractions. A visit to the village makes it obvious just how busy and noisy Burton Agnes can be

Above: The magnificent gatehouse of Burton Agnes Hall was built in 1610 as the main house was being completed.

Left: The Norman Manor House was built *c.* 1170-1180 for Roger de Stutville. The exterior was rebuilt in brick in the seventeenth century.

To the west of Burton Agnes Hall stands the Church of St Martin. This was built *c.* 1125 to 1150 and replaced an earlier church. The chancel was rebuilt in 1730 and there were other repairs in the nineteenth century.

The Blue Bell Hotel at Burton Agnes. In a directory of 1823 William Jefferson was the publican while at the time of the 1901 census Isabella Smith (widow), age forty-seven, was the innkeeper and lived there with her four daughters.

Burton Agnes lies on the southern edge of the Yorkshire Wolds.

Home Farm at Hall Road, Burton Agnes, is a late Georgian farm cottage with sliding sash windows and a hipped roof.

Dave Dickinson working on a design for a motor scooter at his workshop in Burton Agnes. *Image courtesy of Dave Dickinson*

Burton Agnes Railway Station opened on the 6 October 1846 and closed on the 5 January 1970. *Image courtesy of Ben Brooksbank*

Above: Music enthusiasts enjoying a performance at the 2010 Burton Agnes Jazz and Blues Festival. *Image courtesy of Burton Agnes Hall*

Left: Clare Teal performing at the 2010 festival. Sir Michael Parkinson described Clare as, 'One of the best vocal talents to emerge from the UK in a long, long while'. *Image courtesy of Burton Agnes Hall*

for it is located on the A614 and in the summer months holiday traffic adds to the caravan transporters, tractors and other commercial vehicles passing through. This major road through the village has always been a factor in the Burton Agnes story and a directory of 1823 recorded that stagecoaches could be boarded here daily to Beverley, Hull, Bridlington and Scarborough. This coaching trade was curtailed in October 1846 with the opening of the Hull and Bridlington Railway. Burton Agnes Station lay about a quarter of a mile south of the village with station buildings designed by the renowned architect George Townsend Andrews.

Seen as one of the sleepier stations on the line the level crossing at Burton Agnes was the location of a major railway accident on 17 September 1947. The crossing gates were closed to allow an early morning train to Bridlington to pass when an army lorry carrying German prisoners from a nearby POW camp crashed through them and stopped in front of the oncoming locomotive travelling at 55 mph. An enquiry into the ensuing crash said that the accident was the fault of the driver, a British staff sergeant, who had no authority to drive the vehicle since he only held a military licence to drive motorcycles. Twelve people died and the accident report concluded that this tragedy 'was due to careless handling of the lorry by an unauthorised and apparently inexperienced driver'.

In 1968 the Hull to Scarborough railway was under threat of closure with surveys of passenger use being carried out to justify this. In the event the line was saved although lesser-used stations like Carnaby, Lowthorpe and Burton Agnes were dispensed with. Burton Agnes Station closed on 5 January 1970 and the station buildings are now a private house. However the growth of private motoring and a good bus service on the Hull–Driffield–Bridlington route means that the village continues to prosper with Burton Agnes Hall itself being the star attraction.

CHAPTER 27

Aldbrough

Situated five miles along the sandy coast from Hornsea, on the B1244 road, Aldbrough was once one of the largest rural settlements in East Yorkshire. The writer Edward Baines described it, in 1823, as 'a flourishing and very lively village' for around that year the population of Aldbrough Parish stood at over 800 people. The place name is thought to be derived from 'old stronghold' and since the village stands on a ridge of higher ground above the low-lying Holderness Plain it is easy to see the appeal of its location for defence in more turbulent times. Mentioned in the *Domesday Book* as 'Aldenburg' the origins of the village are even older for inside the Church of St Bartholomew (dating from Norman times) is a sundial

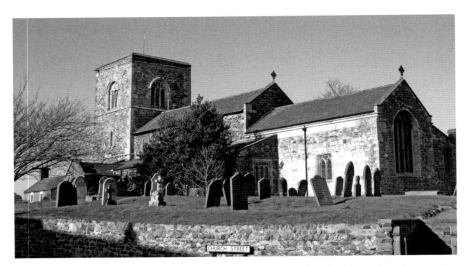

St Bartholomew's Church dates from Norman times and probably replaced an earlier church from the Anglo-Saxon period. The nave and the chancel were restored in 1869-1870. The area around the church was the scene of a weekly market (on Tuesday) and the yearly Aldbrough Fair (late August or early September) from the fourteenth century. The market came to an end at the end of the eighteenth century but St Bartholomew's Fair (mostly for animals) continued until *c.* 1880.

with an Anglo-Saxon inscription that says, 'Ulf ordered this church to be built for his own and Gunware's souls'. Ulf was probably a Danish chieftain and it seems likely that the sundial was moved here from an earlier church.

By the fourteenth century the manor of Aldbrough was held by the de Ros family and in 1332 James de Ros obtained a charter from King Edward the Third to establish a weekly market and an annual two-day fair at the time of the Feast of St Bartholomew (24 August). The fair and the market were held in Church Street and they would have brought together buyers and sellers of livestock, foodstuffs and other merchandise from the surrounding area and further away. The Lords of Holderness and their successors were entitled to charge a toll on stallholders and in 1779 William Constable was charging one old penny for each beast sold and one old penny for each stall.

By the late eighteenth century Aldbrough Fair was held on the 4th of September and from a local newspaper of 1810 we know that the tragic finale of a doomed love affair between a local girl, Ann Ockleton and her spurned suitor, James Whitehead of Preston, was played out there. According to the *Hull Packet* newspaper the young man:

Some time ago paid his addresses to the daughter of Benjamin Ockleton of Aldbrough but had been discarded. He met with her at that place on Tuesday evening and followed her and her aunt into the fields where she had gone to milk cows.

When she continued to reject his attempts at a reconciliation Whitehead assaulted her with a knife. Ann Ockleton, age twenty, survived the attack because of her own courage in wresting the knife away from him and because of the intervention of her aunt who returned to Albrough to summon help. They found Ann 'running down the lane with Whitehead running after her'. John Rogerson, a constable of Aldbrough, took her to her father's house where John Mann, a local surgeon, attended. He found that she had a wound in her throat across the windpipe 'about three and a half inches long and about a quarter of an inch deep' and that there were also cuts to her fingers.

James Whitehead was arrested and sent to York Castle to await trial. He was charged with attempted murder at the York Lent Assizes on 9 March 1811 and initially wished to plead guilty. In the event following advice from the judge, Mr Justice Le Blanc, a plea of not guilty was entered and the trial began. Whitehead had first met Ann Ockleton in December 1809 when they worked together as servants at Hedon. From evidence presented at the trial it appears that as their relationship blossomed Whitehead had visited Ann at her father's house in Aldbrough and that they had became lovers. Unfortunately for Whitehead this affair became a dangerous obsession and when she attempted to end their relationship his mood became dangerous.

The George and Dragon public house dates from the late seventeenth century. The yard had stabling for sixteen horses and there was a coach service to Hull in the early nineteenth century. An advertisement from the *Eastern Counties Herald* in July 1840 read: 'For Sale, George Inn in the occupation of Robert Wreathall'. The public house had its own malt kiln and brewhouse.

Bungalows on Seaside Road at Aldbrough.

Summing up the evidence Judge Le Blanc that there was nothing in law that could 'justify the passions of the prisoner'. The jury soon found Whitehead guilty of attempted murder but recommended mercy. Despite this pleas on his behalf Le Blanc initially sentenced Whitehead to death although he later ordered a reprieve and substituted a sentence of transportation for life.

From an Australian online database we know that James Whitehead was sent to Van Diemen's Land (Tasmania) on 4 June 1812, one of many convicts aboard the sailing ship *Indefatigable*. Whitehead arrived there in October 1812 and was immediately put to work. Life in the new colony was hard and the discipline for even minor offences was brutal with floggings commonplace. Whitehead later went on the run with a gang of other escaped convicts and with a price on their heads they resorted to stealing and killing in order to survive. James Whitehead was the leader of this gang of 'bushrangers' but was killed on 18 May 1815 in a raid on the home of a settler by soldiers who were lying in wait.

At the beginning of the nineteenth century Aldbrough was a typical agrarian community and fourteen farmers were named in a village directory of 1823. The village seems to have been at the centre of the important carrying trade and a Hull directory listed four carriers who provided a service to Aldbrough. By this time Aldbrough's potential to attract visitors was also recognised since the health benefits of bathing and bracing sea air had become fashionable. The Constables of Burton Constable had a teahouse on the cliffs in the 1770s and there was a beer house there by 1832. A large hotel called the Talbot was built shortly after. To bring in the visitors Aldbrough also had an omnibus service from Hull during the holiday season while a local newspaper of June 1836 commented enthusiastically, 'sea bathing has commenced, the sands are good and an excellent road has been made down the cliff'. The Spa Inn (later the Royal) was mentioned from 1846 and there were three lodging houses near the cliff and another in the village while a directory says there was a 'bathing machine proprietor'. In 1840 there was also a short-lived attempt to make Aldbrough attractive to race-goers with Aldbrough Races being advertised.

It was the coming of the railways however that put a curb on Aldbrough's tourist ambitions. The village was not served by them so that when the Hull to Withernsea line opened in 1854 and the Hull to Hornsea railway in 1864 the village lost ground to these upstart rivals. Yet as the Aldbrough School Logbook shows the sea and the sand still had the power to attract day-trippers for an entry from June 1892 recorded a 'holiday this afternoon on account of the Hull Shop Assistants having their annual picnic at the Aldbrough seaside'.

The school logbooks make interesting reading and reveal the kind of attendance problems typical of a rural school in the nineteenth century when children were often expected to undertake farm work and outbreaks of infectious diseases, like diptheria, were an ever-present threat. Discipline at the school could be brutal and in March 1891 the schoolmaster recorded that he had given a thrashing to Robert Tennison for inattention in class during which his cane had snapped.

The war memorial in Church Street.

Seaside Road at Aldbrough.

The post mill in Sandpits Lane, Aldbrough. *Image courtesy of the East Riding Museums Service*

The mill at Carlton Road, Aldbrough was built in the late eighteenth century and ceased operations *c.* 1930. *Image courtesy of the East Riding Museums Service*

ALDBROUGH
RACES.

THURSDAY, August 6th. 1840.

To start at half-past One o'clock in the Afternoon.

A GOOD AND FIRM SAND.

A SUBSCRIPTION CUP,
Or £4.

For Horses of all Ages—Entrance 10s. each.
THREE TO START OR NO RACE.
ALSO,

2 Saddles, 4 Bridles

2 Pair of Spurs, and 4 Hand Whips
TO CONTEND FOR.

The horses to be entered at MR. ROBT. WREATHALL'S, the GEORGE INN, in ALDBROUGH, at or before One o'clock, in the Afternoon.

And on the SATURDAY Evening following,

A HAT, VALUE 10s.

To be run for by Men,

AND GLOVES TO WRESTLE FOR.

Left: A poster advertising Aldbrough Races in 1840. These were to be held on the sands but the uncertainty of the event is indicated by the words 'three to start or no race'. *Image courtesy of the East Riding Archives Service*

Below: The crumbling boulder-clay cliffs of the Holderness coast.

Wentworth House on Seaside Road, Aldbrough *c.* 1910. The building has a mid-eighteenth century staircase and was a hotel from the late 1990s. *Image courtesy of Mark Teale*

Children playing in Cross Street Aldbrough *c.* 1910. *Image courtesy of the East Riding Archives Service*

With the arrival of private motoring and motorbus services from Hull in the 1920s and 1930s Aldbrough saw a resurgence of its tourist industry. An issue of the *Hull Daily Mail* from 29 May 1925, for example, pointed to the advantages of reaching the seaside by bus or charabanc rather than the 'overcrowded and stuffy carriages' of railway trains. The article went on to say:

> One of the pleasantest of bus rides is that from Hull to Aldbrough whose delightful sands make a big appeal at this time of the year.

Holiday homes, some of dubious quality, were built near the cliff and along Seaside Road although the erosion by the sea of Aldbrough's soft boulder-clay cliffs put their long-term future in doubt. When the local historian John Wilson Smith came to the village in the early 1950s he noted:

> On the journey from the village down Seaside Road to the cliff top one sees every description of bungalow from really well built structures down to others made from scraps of old tins and wooden crates. At the Royal Hotel there are extensive grounds containing a motley collection of mean shanties which are let in the summer to campers.

In the twenty-first century Aldbrough remains a lovely and tranquil coastal village yet provides villagers with the things they need through its two shops and three pubs. There is also a youth hall and a village hall that is well used by local people for activities like auctions, table tennis and keep fit.

CHAPTER 28

Sutton-on-Hull

The saying goes that 'absence makes the heart grow fonder' and as someone who spent his formative years of the 1950s and 1960s in Sutton-on-Hull I had almost forgotten what a picturesque and fascinating place it is. When I grew up there, though suburban Hull was fast approaching, it was still recognisable as a distinct village with plenty of open countryside along Wawne Road and Saltshouse Road. Back in the 1950s Tweendykes Road in Sutton remained almost rural and was lit by gas lamps while in the early 1960s I was able to travel by train from the centre of Hull to Sutton passing through other suburban stations, like Botanic Gardens and Stepney, *en route*. My part-time job as a newspaper boy also took me to

Church Street Sutton today.

Sutton Station every Saturday to collect copies of the *Sports Mail* from the train until the Beeching Axe closed the railway in October 1964. More than anything else it was the creation of the Bransholme Estate, from the late 1960s, that helped to absorb the village into the city.

To understand the location and importance of Sutton in the days before Hull even existed it is necessary to look at the topography of the area. The village stood on a ridge of higher ground stretching from Wawne to Bilton and above the level of the surrounding marshes. The place name was probably derived from the Anglo-Saxon settlers of England from the fifth century onwards and may mean 'south farm'. Mentioned in the Domesday Book as Sudtone there was a chapel here occupying the site of the later church although the dead of the village had to be taken to Wawne for burial. It was not until the fourteenth century that the lord of the manor, Sir John de Sutton, decided to replace the chapel with something grander. St James's Church was one of the earliest brick built churches in England. It was built using locally made bricks and stone brought up-river to Stoneferry and then by the Antholme Dyke to Sutton. The church was dedicated in the year 1349, the year of the Black Death, and this great pestilence seems to have delayed further work on the building. The west end and the brick tower were not added until the beginning of the fifteenth century and were built in the Perpendicular Style then fashionable.

Often referred to as Sutton-in-Holderness the village was one of the largest in East Yorkshire and in 1377 as many as 299 adults paid the poll tax. Life here, as elsewhere, was dominated by farming with the cultivated land being on the ridge where the village stood and beyond these arable fields were the marshes and carrs that, when drained, became commons and meadows. An Act of Parliament enclosed the open fields of Sutton in 1763 and in a directory of 1823 eighteen farmers were named along with the usual trades and occupations of self-reliant communities of the time.

The village also had its local officials like the Overseers of the Poor who collected the poor rate from wealthier inhabitants in support of those like widows and orphans who were less fortunate. There was a parish workhouse in Church Street, Sutton for sixteen inmates from 1757 and this was supplemented by charitable bequests such as that provided by Leonard Chamberlain, a Hull draper, and Ann Watson. Their generosity provided hospitals or almshouses for poor widows and among Sutton's wealth of historic buildings is the College built in 1816 at a cost of £1,300 by the Ann Watson trustees. This was provided for the comfort of 'widows and daughters of poor clergymen'.

Another of Sutton's unpaid officials was the parish constable chosen or elected to serve for a year and charged with investigating crimes in the days before the establishment of professional police forces. From documents in the East Riding Archive and newspaper reports of the 1820s we know that Thomas England was a Sutton constable and since the parish covered a large area including Stoneferry

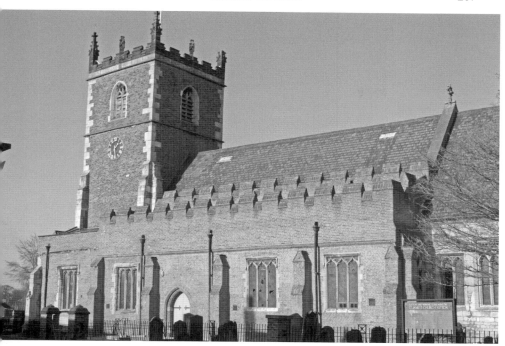

St James's Church in Sutton dates to the mid fourteenth century. It contains the tomb of Sir John de Sutton who fought at the Battle of Crécy in 1346.

Church Street Sutton in 1931 with the Ship Inn (*c.* 1804) on the left. *Image courtesy of the Sutton Resource Centre*

Sutton Station *c.* 1910 after the railway track had been doubled. *Image courtesy of the Sutton Resource Centre*

The blacksmith's in Church Street Sutton *c.* 1900. In 1881 Thomas Calvert was named as the blacksmith but by 1892 his widow, Elizabeth, was running the business. *Image courtesy of the Sutton Resource Centre*

his duties took him beyond the village itself. On 8 February 1825 he secured the conviction of William Morrill of Sculcoates, labourer, for 'having a gaming table and playing with passengers going upon a turnpike road leading from Hull into Holderness'. For his crime Morrill was sentenced to six weeks in the Beverley House of Correction with hard labour. On 18 October 1829 he apprehended William Garton alias Thompson with a sack containing stolen poultry. Garton was sent to prison for three months for his offence.

As the town of Hull began to expand beyond the line of its medieval fortifications after the first dock was opened in 1787 so Sutton became increasingly one of the favoured locations of Hull's merchant class eager to move out into the countryside. This process was encouraged by the arrival of the railway in the village when the Hull & Hornsea line opened in March 1864 for Sutton had a conveniently-located railway station. Until the early 1900s however the railway was a single-track line and this could cause problems if there was an accident. The *Hull Packet* reported on an incident near Sutton Station in November 1865 when the engine of a goods train heading for Hull came off the track causing severe disruption to passenger traffic for some hours. The newspaper wrote critically of the 'almost incredible folly' of the officials at Hull station who dispatched the 5 p.m. train for Hornsea as usual even though they knew the line was blocked. The newspaper reported that on arrival at Sutton Station these passengers were forced to return to Hull.

By looking at old ordnance survey maps, like those to be found on the East Riding Archives website, and using census returns and trade directories it is possible to see the growing importance of Sutton as a residential centre for the well-to-do. A 1910 map of Sutton shows a large mansion on Lowgate called Beech Lawn and in 1892 this was the home of Thomas Bulmer, a seed crusher of the firm Bulmer & Field of High Street Hull. Census returns show that living with him at Beach Lawn in 1881 was his wife, his eight children and one servant. From the mid-nineteenth century new villas were also appearing on Saltshouse Road to the east of the village including Sutton Grange, Tilworth Grange, Risholme Hill and East Mount. The latter was the home of Samuel Priestman (1800-1872) a corn miller and a railway company director. Samuel Priestman was a Quaker and he and his wife Mary Anne brought up eleven children at East Mount. One of these, William Dent Priestman (1847-1936), became a skilled engineer and in 1870 his father, without telling him, paid £3,000 to buy his son a run-down engineering works in Hull called the Holderness Foundry. In partnership with his brother Samuel this was to become the forerunner of the famous Hull engineering company of Priestman Brothers, manufacturers of diggers, dredgers, cranes, and other industrial machinery.

By the late nineteenth century Sutton was a thriving community with chapels for the Weslyeyan Methodists (1859) and the Primitive Methodists (1876) together with a reading room and library paid for by subscription (1882). It also had a National School built in 1859 to provide an elementary education for the

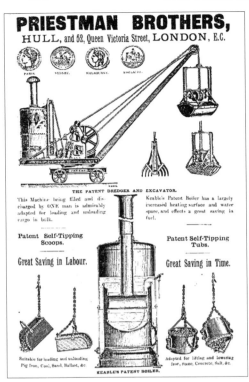

An advertisement for Priestman Brothers of Hull. William Dent Priestman, engineer, spent his childhood years at East Mount, Saltshouse Road, Sutton.

The war memorial at Church Street Sutton.

Jessamine Cottage in Lowgate dates from *c.* 1700.

Ann Watson's College in Sutton dates from 1816. It replaced an earlier hospital in Stoneferry. Ann Watson died in 1721 and left money in her will to provide a hospital for the widows and daughters of poor clergymen.

The ladies of Ann Watson's College *c.* 1900. *Image courtesy of the Sutton Resource Centre*

children of Sutton and Stoneferry. Although this transferred to modern buildings in 1977 the original school building in Church Street is still in use as a Museum and Resources Centre, a remarkable amenity that preserves photographs, artefacts and documents of the old village.

For those who have never seen it a visit to Sutton-on-Hull is therefore to be recommended for this is a place full of charm and character. Its historical and architectural importance was recognised, in 1974, by the granting of conservation area status and it contains ten listed buildings including cottages from the seventeenth and eighteenth centuries.

CHAPTER 29

Airmyn

In an age of modern motor transport and motorways it is easy to forget a time when roads were less preferred than today. Centuries ago Yorkshire's rivers were more widely used to move people and goods because they were more convenient and reliable than the muddy and ill-maintained roads of the time. Towns and villages that had access to water transport were therefore at an advantage and one of these was Airmyn, originally part of the parish of Snaith and of the historic West Riding of Yorkshire. Until the eighteenth century the dead of Airmyn were taken by boat to Snaith to be buried since it was quicker to go by river than by road.

A tinted Edwardian postcard of Airmyn High Street in the early 1900s. *Image courtesy of the East Riding Museums Service*

The name of the village is thought to be derived from the Aire, Yorkshire's longest river, and from *mynne* an old Norse word meaning 'river mouth'. Since the village grew up about half a mile from the Aire's confluence with the Lower Ouse it was ideally placed to develop as a port. Evidence from a court case in 1253 suggests that Airmyn was a planned medieval settlement established by the Abbey of St Mary's at York sometime between the mid twelfth and thirteenth centuries.

Airmyn's heyday as a port came in the eighteenth century when it became a place of transhipment for the Aire & Calder Navigation. They built warehouses, cranes and wharves along the river frontage. Local historian and long-time resident, David Galloway, has written three books on Airmyn and told me of this 'golden age':

> Airmyn's boom period came between 1744 and 1778. It took over from Rawcliffe in this regard because the water is much deeper here and gave easier access for sea-going ships to moor up and unload their cargoes either on to the ten staithes that were built for this purpose or into smaller vessels that could then go upriver to Wakefield or to Leeds. The reason for it all coming to an end in 1778 was that the Selby Canal was built and vessels were able to access the upper reaches of the Aire from the Ouse by travelling the five miles along the new canal.

Once the Selby Canal opened Airmyn's decline was rapid with the riverside coal yard and offices closing in 1779 and a boat-repair yard soon after.

In the early nineteenth century Airmyn was a typical farming community and an estate village of the Percy Family. Like many landowners of the time George Percy, the Earl of Beverley, was generous to the village and paid for the building of a school on High Street in 1834. This Church of England school could accommodate 120 pupils and the vicar was a figure of importance in supervising its management. However in 1855 the newly appointed vicar, the Revd William Hutchinson was soon in disagreement with the schoolmaster, John Watson, over the running of the school and events took a bizarre turn. A story appeared in a York newspaper that the vicar had violently assaulted a young boy called William Fielder for causing a disturbance to his sermon during the church service on Sunday 29 July 1855. The correspondent claimed that the vicar had 'in a violent and passionate manner seized the poor little boy and dragged him with great violence into the vestry' and commenced beating him with his walking stick causing injuries to the boy's arm, ribs and back. The writer, said to be a local farmer called William Dodgson, claimed that the boy's father had subsequently remonstrated with the vicar and threatened legal proceedings.

Two weeks later the newspaper was forced to print a retraction (25 August) having received a letter from the Airmyn Parochial Church Council refuting the allegations and suggesting the article was libellous, malicious and untruthful

A tinted Edwardian postcard of the River Air at Airmyn in the early 1900s. *Image courtesy of the East Riding Museums Service*

The original Airmyn School erected in 1834 by George Percy, Earl of Beverley.

The Percy Arms at Airmyn. It was called the Bay Horse Inn from the late eighteenth century until 1867, before briefly becoming the Beverley Arms and then the Percy Arms. In a directory of 1822 John Cawood was the licensee.

Airmyn's impressive War Memorial Hall was opened in 1993 and completed in 2000.

and arose from 'the malevolence of the schoolmaster of the village who having previously received notice to relinquish his situation has, under a feigned name, adopted this mode of revenge'.

In the early nineteenth century Airmyn possessed the usual trades and occupations of self-reliant villages of the time and in 1822 there were 750 people living there. A directory of the time showed that there were tradesmen like a corn miller, shoemakers, carpenters, grocers and tailors to serve them. Six farmers were also named and a ferry met the need for their workers to cross the river to Little Airmyn and elsewhere since the road journey was seventeen miles via Snaith.

Airmyn Ferry was in existence from at least the early fourteenth century. Historical records from around the year 1311 show 'that Richard, the son of William Newsome, Clerk, gave to the Priory of Drax a sixth part of the ferry at Airmyn, which was given him by Adam, son of Adam de Airmyn, and others, namely John the Carpenter of York and Margaret his wife and William de Garton and Joan his wife'. Two ferrymen, John Hayall and John Muram, were named in the Poll Tax returns of 1379 and were taxed at six old pence instead of the more usual four pence.

By the nineteenth century it was also used as a public ferry and children from Little Airmyn and Newland were ferried across to attend Airmyn School. The route was so busy by 1900 that it was said that the two men operating the ferry 'were hard pressed to cope with the traffic using it'.

The dangerous nature of the ferry crossing is indicated by an accident that took place on 26 February 1880 when the boat capsized and two men were drowned. A local newspaper of the time gave a graphic account of what happened.

A party of about twelve of us left the Hook Sale together and when near Airmyn Mr Tomlinson, the owner of the boat, passed us in company with his brother in a pony and trap. When we got up to the Airmyn clock tower Mr Tomlinson got his pony out of the trap and into the boat. We called out and asked him if he could take us across and he replied he could. Someone called out how many and he said, 'all'. he said the boat could carry five tons. We had all got in but one or two when Mr Tomlinson said ,'jump in lads, we shall be all right.' We all got in but the boat went sideways, struck the landing stage and capsized. It was dark and the moon was not yet up. The tide being so strong it drove me under the water.

At an inquest into the death of one of the men drowned (George Atkinson, aged eighteen) held in July 1880 the jury returned a verdict of 'accidental death'.

In February 1922 there was another ferryboat tragedy when two schoolgirls, returning from a shopping trip to Goole, and a young farm servant were drowned. Four others narrowly escaped a similar fate. The *Hull Daily Mail* reported that a boat had just set off when the keel came into contact with a submerged wire rope.

The ferry at Airmyn existed from at least the early fourteenth century and operated to Little Airmyn across the river. *Image courtesy of Susan Butler / Howdenshire History Website*

The peace-parade at Airmyn in November 1918 to mark the end of the First World War. *Image courtesy of the East Riding Museums Service*

Airmyn Clock Tower paid for by the villagers and built *c.* 1868 in memory of George Percy, Earl of Beverley. *Image courtesy of the East Riding Museums Service*

The vessel then tilted, turned turtle and the 'occupants were all thrown into the water'.

Although there has been a significant growth of new housing in the village since the completion of the M62 motorway to Goole in 1975 Airmyn retains the charm of yesteryear thanks to the preservation of its historic High Street. It is also a village with a thriving sense of community. The Airmyn Memorial Hall is testament to this for this remarkable building is more akin to a sports hall than the usual type of village hall found elsewhere.

CHAPTER 30

Roos

One of the interesting aspects of East Riding villages since the Second World War is how some have hardly grown at all while others have seen a rapid development of modern housing. In 1961 the population of the civil parish of Roos, twelve miles east of Hull, was 631 people but by the time of the 2011 census this had risen to 1,113.

Through the long established village newsletter, the *Rooster*; it is possible to see the growth of Roos in some detail. Between 1976 and 1987, for example, an average of four new houses were built each year and as a 'selected settlement' Roos continued to develop in the years that followed.

All Saints Church at Roos lies at some distance from the modern village. Parts of it date to the thirteenth century. Nearby is the site of Roos Castle or the Manor House. First recorded in the thirteenth century the manor house was probably disused by 1416.

The name Roos is probably derived from 'watery land' and from archaeological discoveries we know there was settlement here in the Iron Age. In 1836 the famous 'Roos Carr figures' were found by some labourers cleaning a ditch and became a major exhibit at the Hull and East Riding Museum. The eight carved figures and a miniature boat in pinewood were probably buried as a religious offering and have been radiocarbon dated to around the mid sixth century BC.

Anyone who has been to Roos will have noticed how far away from the modern-day village its ancient church of All Saints is. This suggests that the original Roos was further south near to the church and to the adjacent moated manor house or castle for this would have afforded the villagers some protection in times of trouble. The building of the church and the castle probably began in the thirteenth century and the latter became the home of the de Ros family. They had been granted the Manor of Roos by Henry the First, king of England from 1100 to 1135, and they continued to be of importance here until the sixteenth century.

For the ordinary folk of Roos their yearly routine would have been dominated by the needs of farming under an open field system of arable and pasture until an act of enclosure was passed in 1783. The manorial court continued to meet until the late nineteenth century and it appointed a number of officials like the pinder who rounded up stray animals and the constable who arrested wrongdoers and brought them before local magistrates for punishment. From records in the East Riding Archive we know that in January 1821 John Ellerby, the village miller, was indicted for rescuing a black mare from the pound at Roos, 'against the will of Robert Suddaby, pinder'.

The unpaid job of policing Roos could also be onerous for in 1808 the village constable, Francis Clapison, made a statement to local magistrates complaining that on Sunday 23 October a 'violent and disorderly concourse of people' estimated at over 200 had unlawfully assembled at Roos and 'great outrages had been committed and officers of the peace insulted'. His statement was supported by that of Thomas Cook who said that his orchard and garden had been entered, trees had been broken down, water tubs overturned, and that his beer casks had been destroyed and thrown into the street.

For those who were caught the criminal code of the time could be extremely harsh. A local newspaper of 24 March 1829 reported on the theft of a donkey, a saddle and other items from William Wright a farmer of Roos. The donkey was eventually tracked down to South End, Hull where it had been sold for fourteen shillings. Initially the crime was blamed on William Close, a former resident of Roos and the nephew of a local farmer. Arrested for four separate felonies he was described at a magistrate's hearing held at the Public Hall in Sculcoates as a 'young boy no more than fifteen or sixteen'. In the event it was another youth, John Maloney, who appeared at the East Riding Quarter Sessions in Beverley on 27 April 1829 to answer the charges. In court it was shown that William Close had been duped into believing the donkey belonged to Maloney and that he was simply

The name-stone of the village erected for the new millennium. It depicts the coat of arms of the de Ros family, lords of the manor of Roos from the twelfth century to the sixteenth century.

The Roos Arms public house and restaurant on Main Street. Parts of the building date to the sixteenth century. In a directory of 1892 William Pickering was named as the licensee but was also a horse breaker.

an unwitting accomplice to the crime. Maloney was found guilty and despite the fact that he was only sixteen he was sentenced to seven years' transportation.

At the time of the 1821 census the parish of Roos had a population of 442 people and a trade directory of that time showed the typical trades and occupations of a rural village. Seventeen farmers were named along with one blacksmith, two wheelwrights, two tailors and five shoemakers. For orphans unable to support themselves or for adults because of factors like sickness, old age or unemployment the Elizabethan Poor Law of 1603 required that the parish overseers make provision. From the overseers accounts of 1827 we can see that the child of Ann Owst was supported by a payment of four shillings a week and that George Ellerby received parish relief of half-a-crown for fifteen weeks. The ratepayers met the cost of this poor relief with a tax on their property and this was set at one shilling and sixpence in the pound for the year 1785. At the South End of the village Robert Bell's property was valued at £354 so he was assessed for poor rates of £26 11s 0d.

The rising cost of relief nationally and the belief that the old system encouraged idleness and reckless breeding among the able-bodied poor led to the passing of the 1834 Poor Law. This made the provision of poor relief in a well-regulated workhouse the preferred option and the aim was to make life there so hard that only the most desperate would seek assistance. Parishes were combined into Poor Law Unions in order to provide a workhouse and Roos became part of the Patrington Poor Law Union in 1836. A new Union Workhouse was built at Patrington in 1837-1838 to house 120 inmates. To minimise the cost of poor relief feckless husbands and fathers who tried to evade their responsibilities were pursued through the courts. On 30 December 1843, for example, Henry Whiting was convicted of deserting his wife and children and of leaving them in the workhouse so that they were then chargeable to the parish of Roos. For this offence he was sentenced to one month in the Beverley House of Correction with hard labour.

Data from the 1881 census and information from a directory of 1892 shows that Roos was a thriving agrarian village in the late nineteenth century. In 1881 the Elms was the home of George Dickinson, age sixty-three, a prosperous farmer employing nine men and three boys. Living with him at the house was his wife, his sister, his son and his two daughters. His son William, age nineteen, was described as 'an undergraduate of Oxford'. George Dickinson was wealthy enough to be able to employ a governess, a cook, a kitchen maid and a housemaid. Another resident of Roos in 1881 and living on Main Street was Robert Jubb, tailor, whose business employed two apprentices.

Another area of change in the nineteenth century was education and important turning point was the passing of an education act in 1870 that established a national framework for the elementary education of children aged five to eleven. At Roos the National School in Pilmar Lane had a new main room built in

The Ella. D. Bridal Studio at Melbourne House, Roos was established in 2004.

Pinfold Cottages at Mill Lane Roos *c.* 1910. *Image courtesy of Roos Parish Council*

Right: The windmill at West Field Roos in the later nineteenth century. *Image courtesy of the East Riding Museums Service*

Below: The children and staff of Roos Church of England School in 1928. *Image courtesy of Roos Parish Council*

Roos Arms, Looking North.

The Roos Arms on Main Street *c.* 1910. *Image courtesy of Roos Parish Council*

1872. However until attendance became both free and compulsory absenteeism remained a problem especially at a time when children were expected to do farm work. In August 1878 for example harvesting duties kept forty-nine pupils away from school.

In the twenty-first century Roos remains a working village centred on agriculture and there are several, mainly arable, farms. It is also a place that attracts newcomers with fresh business ideas and must be unique among Holderness villages in that it has a Bridal Studio at Melbourne House on the Main Street. The continuing success of the village newsletter, the *Rooster* (first published in 1985) shows that Roos retains a thriving community spirit in the new millenium despite its increasing size. Though the village has faced controversial issues in recent times, with the subjects of wind farms and flooding arousing strong feelings, it does retain the character of a close-knit community.

CHAPTER 31

Hotham

It was during the eighteenth century that the landscape of East Yorkshire was transformed by well-to-do families. They were the driving force behind the enclosure of the open fields and common pastures and in the process they created magnificent homes for themselves, often surrounded by fashionable parks and gardens, and became the benefactors of nearby villages. Among the villages that gained were Sledmere, Sewerby, South Dalton and Hotham. The latter is a picturesque community, twelve miles southwest of Beverley, and is a place renowned for its stately home of Hotham Hall and the extensive parkland that separates the village from nearby North Cave.

Hotham Hall is a Grade 2 listed building. It was built around 1720 with later additions.

Like so many East Riding villages the name Hotham comes to us from Anglo-Saxon times and means 'shelter'. The location of the village in a shallow valley and close to Hotham Beck helps to explain both the name and its appeal when a ready supply of drinking water was essential. Archaeological discoveries show that Hotham was a long-established place of habitation since flint tools have been found in its fields while in 2006 the building of a pipeline unearthed a previously un-recorded Bronze-Age barrow on a hilltop east of Hotham. Archaeologists have also unearthed the remains of an iron-age barrow close to the village and with a Roman road from Petuaria (Brough) to Eboracum (York) running nearby it is easy to speculate that this was a favoured location of Romano-Britons too.

In the years that followed Hotham continued to be a place of settlement. It was mentioned in the Domesday Survey of 1086 although the value of the village had declined sharply after the Norman invasion when King William's Harrying of the North meant its lands were 'laid waste'. As with most villages the oldest surviving building is the church. The Church of St Oswald has a chancel, a nave and a massive tower dating from Norman times. The church was restored in 1755 and there was further work on the fabric in the later nineteenth century. A major restoration took place in 1904.

In common with other East Riding villages most of Hotham's population would have been engaged in farming and other rural occupations under an open field system and subject to the same natural calamities experienced elsewhere. One of these was the Black Death of 1349, one of the most devastating pandemics in human history. Its effect on Hotham can be judged by the fact that the tax assessment for the village was reduced by fifty per cent in 1354.

One of the most significant events in the history of the village came in 1719 when William Burton purchased the manor of Hotham. Soon after he built Hotham Hall and there were further improvements, like a pavilion in 1772, to this magnificent residence. The purchase of a nearby estate in 1773 enabled the Burtons to create extensive parklands to the south and one of the great joys of a visit to the area is a walk through these from Hotham to North Cave.

Two of the later occupants of Hotham Hall, Robert Christie Burton (1784-1822) and Henry Burton Peters (1795-1875), had political ambitions to be elected as a Member of Parliament for nearby Beverley. To win one of the two seats there they would have needed their considerable wealth for in the early nineteenth century this was one of the most corrupt boroughs in England; it was commonplace for election results to be influenced by bribery, threats and sharp practice of all kinds. Paying money to the electors, although illegal, was widespread and most candidates escaped punishment. Large sums were spent on the travelling and living expenses of voters who lived outside the town while on polling day those with the franchise expected the candidates to provide food and drink. Robert Christie Burton was elected for Beverley in 1818 despite being in prison for debt at the time. He was represented at the poll by his uncle and as an elected MP used

The gatehouse of Hotham Hall

A seat in Parliament was greatly prized by the beginning of the nineteenth century even though MPs were unpaid. A seat in Parliament conveyed social status and power. Credit: Murray Close © 2006 Bristol Bay Productions (from Amazing Grace, a Samuel Goldwyn/Roadside Attractions Film.)

the legal defence of 'parliamentary privilege' to secure his release from prison and to evade his creditors. However when he was defeated two years later he decided to leave his debts behind by moving to Paris.

Even more colourful was the life of Henry Burton Peters. He came from a wealthy merchant family and achieved early notoriety by seducing the wife of an army officer, Sarah Clithoroe, and eloping with her to France in December 1817. They married in June 1819 and later moved to Hotham Hall when Sarah inherited the estates of her feckless brother, Robert Christie Burton. When the father of Henry Burton Peters died in 1827 he inherited the considerable sum (by nineteenth century standards) of £7,000 a year and used his wealth to secure his election at Beverley in 1830. One of the features of elections at that time was that there was no secret ballot; the way that people had voted was recorded in a polling book. A newspaper account of the time shows that on Election Day the candidates were well aware how well, or badly, they were doing before the poll closed. The *Hull Packet* of 3 August 1830 said:

> The election for Beverley took place on Saturday last. The candidates were Henry Burton of Hotham, Capel Cure and Daniel Sykes. Mr Burton took the lead and in the early part of the day Mr Cure's votes outnumbered those of Mr Sykes.

The result was declared at about 7 p.m. with Burton and Sykes winning the election and was followed by the ceremony of 'chairing the members' with excited crowds of spectators watching the triumphal procession of Burton and Sykes carried aloft on chairs decorated with silk and ostrich feathers.

This was just one of the expenses borne by the candidates. The election accounts of Burton make fascinating reading and show a mass of payments to people like musicians (£287 5s 0d), flag carriers (£94 10s 0d) and 'men for assisting the infirm to the poll' (£2 0s 0d). Of course it is open to question how far these expenses were really disguised bribes. Whatever the truth, Burton's accounts show that he spent £3,200 on his election in 1830 and the following year he was forced to fight another expensive contest at Beverley. Henry Burton's generosity also extended to Hotham itself and from the *York Herald* of 13 March 1847 we learn that:

> Mr and Mrs Burton of Hotham Hall are now freely distributing coals and soup to the necessitous poor of Hotham.

When Burton's wife died in 1869 ownership of Hotham Hall and her estates reverted to her son by her first marriage, Colonel Edward Clitheroe, and he continued to exert a powerful patronage over the village. Census returns and trade directories reveal the typical trades and occupations of a rural village in the later nineteenth century. The 1881 census shows the presence at Snake Hall Farm

Right: A Beverley Poll Book of 1830. The voters were anxious that there should always be three candidates for Beverley's two seats since this would ensure a disputed election and the paying of bribes. The Poll Book shows the three candidates were Henry Burton, Daniel Sykes and Capel Cure. The electors arrived from places other than Beverley (at the candidates expense) to cast their votes openly. Since the poll books were published after the election it was easy to check how people had voted and this could lead to intimidation and dismissal from employment.

Below: A painting by William Hogarth called 'Chairing the Member' indicates the violence that often accompanied elections.

A Copy of the Poll.

VOTERS' NAMES.

☞ The Persons whose places of Residence are not mentioned, live in or near Beverley.

A.	CANDIDATES.		
	BUR.	SYK.	CUR.
Abbott John, innkeeper	306		176
Abbott William, cordwainer	281	·	155
Abbott Thomas, ditto	599		381
Abbott Jonathan, mariner	790		490
Acklam William Etty, currier, *Hull*	196		
Acklam George, cordwainer, *Seaton*	94	44	
Acklam James Leighton, East India House Commodore, *London*	755	498	
Acklam Stephen, gentleman		378	
Acklam James, cordwainer, *Friday-thorpe*	943	638	
Ackrill William, innkeeper	433		267
Ackrill Esau, gun-maker	471		296
Adamson William, potter	75	·	
Adamson Richard, breeches-maker		412	
Adamson Thomas, bleacher, *Harrogate*	95		61
Akester William, cordwainer	378		231
Akester William, jun. ditto	260		145
Akester Robert, shipwright, *Hull*	217	113	
Alcroft Joseph, blacksmith, *ditto*	378		368

Park Cottage at Hotham was built of limestone.

This former Methodist Chapel is now a private house.

The Church of St Oswald dates from Norman times.

The Hotham Arms is an important focal point of the village.

Left: The war memorial at Hotham.

Below: The Main Street at Hotham on a Spring Day.

Baker's Cottage at Hotham.

A walk through the park of Hotham Hall is a popular activity for the people of North Cave.

The Cottage on Main Street (formerly known as Park Street)

of Charles Holt a farmer of 100 acres employing two men while elsewhere in Hotham lived Benjamin Wilson, a thirty-six-year-old domestic tailor and George Balderson a forty-year-old bricklayer. A directory of 1892 reveals that Hotham had its own National School attended by about thirty children. This was the scene of shocking events in June 1894 when the schoolteacher, Mary Wright, was attacked with a knife by her husband. The Wrights' three children who had rushed into the street in their nightclothes had raised the alarm around 7.30 p.m. Witnesses found William Wright sat astride his wife in a bedroom attacking her savagely and reported that she had told them he was 'out of his mind'. It seems the courts agreed with her assessment. Charged with attempted murder in December 1894 at York Assizes the jury found that William Wright was of 'unsound mind'. It was ordered that he be detained during 'his Majesty's pleasure'.

Hotham Church of England School closed in 1948 reflecting the general decline in the population. In 1901 the number of people in the village was 305 but by 1971 the population had fallen to 266. As a history of the village published in 1991 explained:

The Second World War marked a watershed in the social and economic life of Hotham. The craftsmen and shopkeepers departed, the 'Big House' no longer employed so many people, farming became mechanised and in 1989 the last shop and post office closed.